POLICY MAKING IN TRADE UNIONS

Policy Making in Trade Unions

The T&GWUs policy on decasualisation of dock labour

MICHAEL P. JACKSON
School of Management
University of Stirling

Avebury

Aldershot · Brookfield USA · Hong Kong · Singapore · Sydney

Published by

Avebury
Gower Publishing Company Limited
Gower House
Croft Road
Aldershot
Hants GU11 3HR
England

Gower Publishing Company
Old Post Road
Brookfield
Vermont 05036
USA

Printed in Great Britain by
Billing & Sons Ltd, Worcester

ISBN 1 85628 101 9

Contents

Preface

This book is the result of a longstanding interest in both industrial relations on the docks and trade union leadership. In an earlier book, <u>Labour Relations on the Docks,</u> I tried to sketch out some of the main events in the history of the port transport industry. This book is much more focussed and might be of interest to those who are not actually concerned with the specifics of the case study but are looking at the debate over the relationship between union leaders and members.

Much of the work in the preparation of this book has been undertaken by Jennifer Burns, Moira Taylor and Lynne McNaughton, and I am grateful to them for all of their help.

Introduction

Industrial relations in the port transport industry regularly have attracted the attention of the general public and academics alike. In part, this is because the industry stands in such an economically sensitive position; in part, it is because dock workers have developed a reputation for militancy; but, also, in part it is because the conditions of work in the industry until relatively recently were a major cause for concern.

Moves to alleviate the worst effects of the casual system of employment on the docks date back to the end of the nineteenth and the beginning of the twentieth centuries. These moves continued until 1967 when dock work was officially decasualised, although residual problems remained after that date. Throughout this period, the moves found the support of a number of influential union leaders, from the 1920s, principally from the Transport and General Workers' Union. However, the support of union leaders was not always matched by rank and file union members. On occasions, union members openly opposed union policy and such opposition is one part of the explanation for the establishment and extension of rival organisations claiming the allegiance of workers in the industry.

Of course, union members who opposed union policy in the Transport and General Workers' Union, like any other union, had a number of ways of expressing this opposition through constitutional channels. They could have sought to change policy and displace union leaders with whom they disagreed. However, the literature on union internal democracy suggests that despite the constitutional arrangements, disaffected members may face difficulties in getting union policy changed, and even if there is majority support for their view, they may not win the day. In many situations, in practice, it is impossible to tell whether or not there is such majority support. Union members as a whole are only balloted infrequently on policy issues in most unions, and elections for senior officials cannot always be tied down to one policy debate. Anyway, such ballots and elections often only attract a low poll.

It is by no means unusual, therefore, for union members who disagree with union policy on a particular matter, whether they be a majority or minority, to pursue their opposition through other than constitutional means. The means adopted vary greatly. Nevertheless, some attention has been focused on this matter by students of industrial relations who have been concerned to see how union leaders react to such challenges.

This book focuses on the conflicts that occurred between union leaders and rank and file members in the port transport industry. Attention is concentrated specifically on the Transport and General Workers' Union. The aim is to see the form that the conflict took and the way it was dealt with. In this context, the union leaders referred to are the national leaders. They are a changing and less than precise group, but centre around the General Secretary and the other national full-time officials (who in practice gain their authority through him), and the national executive of the union who have responsibility for general policy when the Union's delegate conference is not in session. This is not to suggest that the "union leaders" so described are necessarily a homogeneous group, for at times there are policy as well as personal conflicts within the group. For example, there was one occasion in the post-Second World War period when the General Secretary of the Transport and General Workers' Union publicly rebuked the national docks officer. On occasions these strains within the leadership may be used to effect by disaffected members. Nevertheless, in the case under discussion, generally it is possible to talk about a policy which was approved of by the union leadership. Frequently the main inspiration and direction of the policy has been the responsibility of the General Secretary, but it would be inaccurate in this context simply to talk about one leader.

It is not claimed that this is a study of internal union democracy. There are two reasons for this. First, the notion of democracy in this context is the source of dispute and it is not intended to enter into a discussion of definitions in an extensive fashion. Second, a study of internal democracy would demand a much more detailed analysis of constitutional mechanisms than is attempted. The focus of this study is narrower; it is on policy making and the conflict that can occur between union leaders and members over established policy. This is part of the debate on internal democracy but not all of it.

The analysis of the disputes between union leaders and members over policy on the decasualisation of dock labour is based on a variety of sources of information. The period under discussion is a lengthy one and therefore necessarily much of the information is from documentary sources. These include minutes of meetings of a number of unions, principally, but not simply, of the Transport and General Workers Union, papers prepared within the union and by individuals, the reports of official inquiries, and reports in newspapers and the like. Discussions were held with a number of individuals who were able to supplement the documentary evidence, including some who held senior positions in the Transport and General Workers Union for part of the period under discussion. However, no attempt was made to systematically survey opinion as such.

The structure of the book has been arranged so that the case of the policy of the Transport and General Workers Union on the decasualisation of dock labour can be seen in the context of a more general discussion of policy making in trade unions. Thus, the next chapter reviews existing literature on internal democracy and policy making in trade unions, in its concluding pages paying specific attention to what writers have said about the resolution of open conflict between union members and leaders. The following five chapters examine the development of policy relating to the decasualisation of dock labour in chronological order. In each case, the main events are reported and the evidence of the role and reactions of union leaders and members is reviewed. The last two chapters call attention to the implications that might be drawn from the case of the Transport union's policy on the decasualisation of dock labour. The first of these chapters concentrates on the specific while the second broadens to the more general implications.

1 Internal democracy and policy making in trade unions

The Webbs View of the Transition from Primitive to Representative Democracy

As long ago as the end of the nineteenth century, the Webbs[1] recognised that policy making in trade unions had passed from the hands of the membership directly to representative bodies and organisations. They discussed this change in terms of primitive and representative democracy. Primitive democracy existed in the local trade clubs of the eighteenth century. Policy was made directly by all members: "The members in each trade, in general meeting assembled, themselves made the regulations, applied them to particular cases, voted the expenditure of funds, and decided on such action by individual members as seemed necessary for the common wealth".[2] Sometimes such clubs appointed officers, but when they did so they were chosen in rotation and for particular meetings only. When it became necessary to appoint a committee to carry out certain important tasks, again the members of the committee were chosen in rotation.

The Webbs summarised the operation of primitive democracy in the early trade clubs in the following way:

> The early trade club was thus a democracy of the most rudimentary type, free alike from permanently differentiated officials, executive council or representative assembly. The general meeting strove itself to transact all the business and grudgingly delegated any of its functions either to officers or to committees. When this delegation could not longer be avoided, the expedients of rotation and short periods of service were used "to prevent imposition" or any undue influence by particular members. In this earliest type of trade union democracy we find, in fact, the most childlike faith not only that "all men are equal", but also that "what concerns all should be decided by all."[3]

Such a method of decision and policy making was obviously only compatible with small scale operation.[4]   However, the Webbs argued that it was not so much the scale of operation as the "exigencies of their warfare with the employers"[5] that led trade unions to depart from their model of primitive democracy.   The Webbs also noted, though, the great reluctance with which trade unions moved from the earlier model.   In most cases the development was far from deliberate but evolved unconsciously out of piecemeal decisions designed to deal with a particular situation.   Throughout the nineteenth century trade unions tried to devise ways of ensuring that officials gained only very restricted power;   one such way was the use of the referendum to determine all important questions.   Ironically, the Webbs argued that it was the impracticability of devices like the referendum that led to the final break with primitive democracy.

The Webbs, thus, were able to note that by the end of the nineteenth century, although the "old theory of democracy is still an article of faith, and constantly comes to the front when any organisation has to be formed for brand-new purposes", trade union constitutions have undergone a silent revolution.

The old ideal of the Rotation of Office among all members in succession has been practically abandoned.   Resort to the aggregate meeting diminishes steadily in frequency and importance.   The use of the Initiative and the Referendum has been tacitly given up in all complicated issues, and gradually limited to a few special questions on particular emergencies.   In their place "we have the appearance in the Trade Union world of the typically modern form of democracy, the elected representative assembly, appointing and controlling an executive committee under whose direction the permanent official staff performs its work".[6]

The Webbs spent some time looking in detail at the way "representative democracy" had been established in one union, the Amalgamated Association of Operative Cotton-Spinners. They described the way that legislative power was vested in a parliament, comprised of representatives from the various provinces and districts.   This parliament elected the General Secretary (the senior executive officer) and an executive council of thirteen members, of whom seven had to be working spinners and six were usually permanent officials.   The six permanent officials, in turn, formed a sub-council and undertook most of the daily administration of the union.

The Webbs spent so long examining the workings of this particular union because they believed that it provided a model for representative democracy in trade unions.   They said: "We have watched the working of this remarkable constitution during the last seven years, and we can testify to the success with which both efficiency and popular control are secured". Efficiency was secured by the employment of highly trained staff while popular control was ensured by the real supremacy of the elected representatives.

> For the "Cotton-Spinners' Parliament" is no formal gathering of casual members to register the decrees of a dominant bureaucracy.   It is, on the contrary, a highly organised deliberative assembly, with active representatives from the different localities, each alive to the distinct, and somewhat divergent, interests of his own constituents.   Their eager participation shows itself in constant "party meetings" of the different sections, of which the officers and workmen from each district consult together as to the line of policy to pressed upon the assembly.[7]

The Webbs contrasted the organisation adopted by the Cotton Spinners with that adopted by other unions.   Many permitted the membership to elect officers and the executive council directly, not through an intermediate agency, such as the Cotton Spinners' Parliament.   The Webbs argued that direct election led either to constant fighting between members of the executive and officers or to a coalition between executive members and officers against the rank and file.   In the case of the former, the union suffered because of inefficiency;   in the case of the latter, the union suffered because it became little more than a dictatorship of the officers.[8]

The Webbs' review of the transition from primitive to representative democracy, then, was a cautionary tale, but essentially an optimistic one.[9]   Size meant that it was no longer possible in the majority of cases for union members directly to make all decisions and policy of the union;   however, providing certain guidelines were adhered to, representative institutions could be established which would enable the members to gain the benefits of scale, yet retain an important degree of influence over general union policy, if not detailed decision making.

A More Pessimistic View

The essential optimism of the Webbs contrasts starkly with the pessimism of another major writer of the same period.   Michels examined the workings of voluntary associations, including trade unions,[10] and concluded that they were dominated by small cliques, or by oligarchy.   Rank and file members, Michels argued, had little or no say in policy making in trade unions;   policy was made by, and for the benefit of, a small group of permanent officials and leaders.

Michels' thesis was developed after a study of the German Social Democratic Party.   The choice of this organisation was not accidental;   Michels aimed to see the extent to which an organisation that had the extension of democracy as one of its principal aims operated internally on a democratic basis.

The development which is central to Michels' thesis is "the need for organisation".   Michels argued that in order to achieve their aims organisations like political parties and trade unions needed to do more than merely collect large numbers of members.   They needed to operate efficiently and this inevitably meant the development of some kind of organisation, the election or appointment of leaders and officials.

The Webbs' and Michels' accounts do not differ substantially up to this point.   However, they diverge dramatically later, for, while the Webbs believed that it was possible, providing certain procedures were adopted for the rank and file member to control officials and leaders (and thus ultimately to control policy), Michels argued that such a position was untenable. The leaders and officials have at their disposal a whole armoury of weapons which enables them to dominate the rank and file members and determine policy irrespective of the members' wishes.   Thus, Michels argued:

> The leaders possess many resources which give them an almost insurmountable advantage over members who try to change policies.   Among their assets can be counted (a) superior knowledge, e.g. they are privy to much information which can be used to secure assent for their programme;   (b) control over the formal means of communication with the membership ... and (c) skill in the art of politics.

The domination of the bureaucratic leaders is also facilitated according to Michels by what he termed "the incompetence of the masses".   Few members attend meetings of the organisation;   "the pulls of work, family, personal leisure activities, and the like severely limit the amount of actual time and psychic energy which the average person may invest in membership groups".[12]   Further, few members have the level of education and "general sophistication" necessary to participate fully in the affairs of the organisation.

According to Michels, then, oligarchy was a natural consequence of organisation.   This is summed up in his famous statement; "It is the organisation which gives birth to the domination of the elected over the electors, of the mandatories over the mandators, of the delegates over the delegators. Who says organisation, says oligarchy".[13] Thus, in so far as organisation was essential for a voluntary association to achieve its aims, oligarchy was inevitable in that association, no matter what the intention of the founders or what the philosophy embraced by the association.

However, Michels went further than merely indicating that policy in trade unions would be determined by an oligarchy. He also indicated the factors that would be taken into account in determining that policy. The oligarchy that determines policy develops special interests and aims. "By a universally applicable law, every organ of the collectivity, brought into existence through the need for the division of labour, creates for itself, as soon as it becomes consolidated, interests peculiar to itself". These interests are always conservative, "and in a given political situation these interests may dictate a defensive and even reactionary policy'.[14] Not only will these interests differ from those of the rank and file member ("the interests of the working class demand a bold and aggressive policy"[15]) but the policy adopted will be the opposite of that demand both by the rank and file and by the original aims of the association.

Interestingly Michels argued that in the trade union movement "the authoritative character of the leaders and their tendency to rule democratic organisations on oligarchic lines are even more pronounced than in the political organisations". As a result, he argued that it is even easier in the trade union than in the political organisation "for the officials to initiate and to pursue a course of action disapproved of by the majority of workers they are supposed to represent. It suffices here to refer to the two famous decisions of the trade union congress at Cologne in 1905. In one of these the leaders declared themselves to be opposed (in opposition to the views of the majority) to the continued observance of the 1st May as a general labour demonstration of protest. In the second, the discussion of the general strike was absolutely forbidden. By these and similar occurrences the oligarchical practices of the leaders are sufficiently proved, although some writers continue to dispute the fact".[16]

One of the main criticisms of subsequent Marxist writers of the Michels thesis has been that Michels only considered organisations in a capitalist society. It is not surprising, so such critics argue, that the masses are uninterested and unable to participate in the affairs of the organisation for they have never been encouraged to do so. In a capitalist society, education and training are linked to wealth, with the result that the mass of people are denied access to them. However, in a socialist society, the position will be different; education and training will be available (to all, and all will be encouraged to participate in decision making.[17] This view is probably best expressed by Bukharin:

> (Under socialism) what constitutes an eternal category in Michels' presentation, namely the "incompetence of the masses" will disappear, for this incompetence is by no means a necessary attribute of every system; it likewise is a product of the economic and technical conditions, expressing themselves in the general cultural being and in the educational conditions. We may say that in the society of the future there will be a colossal overproduction of organisers, which will nullify the "stability" of the ruling groups.[18]

A similar point has been made more recently by another writer. Lane has argued that the tendency towards oligarchy in trade unions, "has never been more than a tendency". Crucially, he states, that where oligarchy exists "it is attributable to the nature of trade unionism in a capitalist environment".[19]

Michels seems to have anticipated this criticism to some extent. He argued that while socialist parties cannot deny the existence of oligarchy they endeavour to explain it by suggesting that it is "the outcome of a kind of atavism in the mentality of the masses, characteristic of the youth of the movement". They go on to argue, he noted, that the socialist regime "will soon restore them the health, and will furnish them with all the capacity necessary for self-government".[20] However, Michels argued that this position is built on a misunderstanding of the nature of the problem.

> The objective immaturity of the mass is not a mere transitory phenomenon which will disappear with the progress of democratization "au lendemain du socialisme". On the contrary, it derives from the very nature of the mass as mass, for this, even when organized, suffers from an incurable incompetence for the solution of diverse problems which present themselves for solution - because the mass "per se" is amorphous, and therefore needs division of labour, specialization, and guidance.[21]

Support for Michels

The Michels thesis has been re-examined in a number of different contexts. However, perhaps the best known re-examination in a trade union setting is that of Lipset, Trow and Coleman.[22] They deliberately chose to examine in detail a case where Michels' thesis did not seem to fit. "In this", they said, "our purpose is not, of course, to refute Michels or other previous workers in this area, but rather to refine and build on their insights and findings".[23] The case study they examined was that of the International Typographical Union.

In summary Lipset et al argued that democracy had been maintained in the I.T.U. because of the survival of an organised opposition in the union which prevented any one group from gaining control. The organised opposition had survived, they argued, because of a number of unusual circumstances which could be seen by examining the history of the union and the context in which it operated. Five such unusual circumstances might be highlighted. First, members of the I.T.U. were more interested and involved in the work of the union than one might have expected. This was partly because of the nature of the craft of printing; the high status of printers and their irregular hours of work had led to the creation of a strong occupational community, which in turn had fostered the desire of printers to participate in the affairs of their union. Second, the borderline or marginal status of printing between the middle and working class meant that there were different groups with different values within the union. Third, a fairly high proportion of the printing trades were organised before the union was formed and as a result the various sections of the union had a long history of autonomy which led them to resist strongly efforts to create a centralised structure. Fourth, as a result of earlier problems, the union had developed a number of devices designed to enable the whole of the membership to participate in major aspects of decision making; these include the election of officers by the whole of the membership and provisions for referenda of the membership. Fifth, the results of the elections were accepted; ruling groups had not tried to preserve their position after an election defeat by "illegal means".

Lipset et al were at pains to point out that the I.T.U. was atypical of most trade unions. Organised opposition had only survived because of "favourable dice throws". In most unions such conditions would not exist and unions would be dominated by an oligarchy. They concluded:

> This study has not "disproved" Michels' theory; rather, in a sense, it has given additional empirical support to his analysis of the connection between oligarchy as a political form and the overwhelming power held by the incumbent officers of most private organisations, by demonstrating that where an effective and organized

opposition does exist, it does so only because the incumbent administration does not hold a monopoly over the resources of politics.[24]

One of the best known case studies of the internal organisation of a British trade union is Goldstein's analysis of the Transport and General Workers Union.[25] Completed in the early 1950s, it centred on membership participation in union affairs and policy making. Goldstein argued that there was overwhelming evidence that most rank and file members had little or no interest or involvement in the affairs of the Transport and General Workers Union. One of the pieces of evidence cited was membership turnover. "A large turnover", he argued, "is both evidence and a principal cause of apathy within an organisation".[26] He noted that during the period 1935 to 1947 membership turnover averaged 33.3 percent of the total national membership of the union. He stated: 'Though impossible to ascertain from the data presented here, a large proportion of these lapses can be attributed to indifference on the part of the individual, i.e. a failure to identify himself with the Union to which he belongs'.[27] A second piece of evidence quoted was the Union's electoral system and record. He noted that few members regularly exercised their right to vote in elections and commented:

> In fact, the Transport and General Workers Union's electoral system is in practice as much a cause of apathy as election returns are an index of it. The Union is so diseased by apathy that corruption at the ballot box may go unnoticed by a large majority of rank and file members.[28]

He also calculated that because of the high turnover of membership and the extent of arrears of subscriptions about 80 percent of union members were ineligible to stand for official positions in the Union at any one time.

However, the crucial evidence presented was a case study of participation at branch level. Goldstein argued that:

> The extent to which the union can claim that it is a representative democracy is dependent upon the amount and degree of participation of rank and file members at Branch level. Without participation there can be no democracy. Without democracy the control of this powerful state within(a state in the hands of an irresponsible few.[29]

When he came to describe branch life in detail Goldstein painted a picture remarkably close to the most pessimistic of the possibilities outlined above. He noted that branch meetings were held regularly for a membership that was so large that if the majority were to attend, full participation would be impossible. In fact, he said, meetings only attracted a handful of members who dominated branch life. The union civil servants, he said, were in a position to, and often did, "usurp the policy-determining functions assigned in theory to elected representatives". Goldstein concluded that the "features of the Branch disclosed by this mass of descriptive material are those of an oligarchy parading in democracy's trappings".[30]

Elements of the Michels thesis can also be supported by reference to a host of other studies. For example, many writers have referred to the lack of participation of members in branch affairs. Thus, Roberts[31] suggested that attendance at branch meetings fell into the range of 3% to 15% with a concentration between 4% and 7%; a Political and Economic Planning survey[32] found that attendance at branch meetings ranged from 2% to 30% of the membership; Goldthorpe and Lockwood[33] discovered that only 7% of their car workers attended branch meetings regularly and the Workplace Industrial Relations Survey[34] suggested that on average only about 7% of their extensive sample of union members attended branch meetings. Some writers have tried to account for the differences in attendance between unions and between different types of members; Seidman et al[35] drew up a typology of union members, while Lumley[36] has noted that attendance at branch meetings is often greater amongst white collar than blue collar members. Others have suggested ways of increasing membership attendance; for instance, Cole[37] argued that attendance at branch meetings might be greater if more branches were based on the place of work rather than area of residence and the Workplace Industrial Relations Survey[38] found that attendance at workplace branch meetings was significantly higher than for their sample as a whole. However, Davis[39] in his study of the Australian Metal Workers Union noted that the increase in the number of workers commuting to work may have made occupationally based branches less effective than they were and anyway few have argued that participation in branch affairs is, or in the foreseeable future could be, more than a minority pursuit.

A number of writers have noted that not only are branch meetings attended by a small minority of members, but also that the officials who run the branch are elected by a similarly small proportion; thus, Cyriax and Oakeshott stated that branches "are nearly always dominated by an inner clique which does the work and is voted into office by a small percentage of the membership".[40] An International Labour Office survey[41] of trade unionism in Britain noted that voting figures can be higher on contentious issues and it is worth recording that recent ballots amongst members of the National Trade Union of Mineworkers on industrial action achieved very high returns.[42] The NUM also achieved an 80% turnout for the election of their President in 1981. In many cases, though, voting figures are low for the election of both national and local officials; for example, the turnout in the election of the AUEW(E) General Secretary in 1982 was 18.6% while the turnout for the executive elections for ASTMS in the same year varied from 2% to 7%. In many cases local officials and shop stewards will be elected unopposed. For example, McCarthy[43] found that 71% of shop stewards were elected unopposed and a later study, the 1984 Workplace Industrial Relations survey,[44] found that in most cases shop stewards were elected without a contest.

Writers, like Sayles and Strauss[45] and Tabbenbaum and Kahn[46] have argued that there is a greater opportunity for democratic processes to operate at the branch than at the national level. At the local level there is a much closer contact between leaders and rank and file members than could ever be the case at the national level of a major union. However, it is often argued that the major decisions on union policy are taken not at the local, but at the national level though there are, of course, considerable variations in the extent of centralisation or decentralisation of decision taking from union to union.

A number of other studies have concentrated on leadership in trade unions. Wright-Mills has shown[47] how union leaders can divert trade unions from their central aims; union leaders can become "managers of discontent". In another study,[48] the same author has referred to national union leaders as part of the "power elite",[49] while Coleman[50] has looked at how union leaders manage to maintain the facade of democracy when their organisations have long since ceased to be subject to democratic control. Many studies have highlighted the excesses of American union leaders. Hall[51] shows how bribery, corruption and violence have been used by some American union leaders to defeat rank and file critics; specific reference is made to the case of Jock Yabloski who was killed in January 1970 after his challenge for the presidency of the United Mineworkers union. Romar has examined the career of Hoffer in the International Brotherhood of Teamsters in a similar fashion, while Roberts has commented that:

> In some unions the rights of members have been flagrantly violated by union leaders intent on keeping power at all costs. In others, the authority, prestige and monopoly

of the unions medium of communication is combined to make any successful challenge to the established position of union leaders a remote possibility.[52]

In another publication Roberts argued that American union leaders formed a self perpetuating elite; "Defeat is not accepted as a risk inherent in the job, as it is by any democratic politician. Not only do incumbents refuse to accept the possibility of personal defeat, but accession to office of their chosen successor has now become a matter of prestige".[53] A related issue, is the extent to which union leadership has now become a "profession". Union leaders now move more frequently than in the past between unions and some writers have argued that this has led to an identification with an occupation rather than with a particular union.[54] Considerable concern has also been expressed about the internal procedures for arbitrating in disputes between individual members and the union leaders. Kerr[55] has been particularly critical of the ways unions have failed to develop adequate procedures to guarantee the rights of the individual and his concern has been echoed by Summers[56] and Leiserson.[57] All put forward the view that unions have too much power over the work environment to be permitted to operate without adequate procedures guaranteeing individual freedom. Broomwich[58] surveyed the constitutions of seventy American unions and noted deficiencies in their procedures for dealing with the disciplining of members, disputes over election results and the like.

Nevertheless, it is important to recognise that despite the wealth of evidence available, many writers, and even many of the writers already quoted, are not as pessimistic about union democracy, and the ability of rank and file members to influence policy, as might be imagined. This is true, for instance, of the authors of the case studies of the International Typographical Union and the Transport and General Workers Union. Thus, Lipset argued that although,

> the events and conditions in the ITU are unique and are rarely found in trade unions or other voluntary large social organizations generally, it would be foolhardy to predict that democratic processes cannot develop elsewhere. The specific factors which underly ITU democracy are not likely to be duplicated elsewhere; but the very great variety of factors present in the situation suggests that democratic processes may develop under quite different conditions and take quite different forms.[59]

Lipset concluded by suggesting that the ITU, if it doesn't provide a model, should provide a touchstone against which the internal organisation of other unions can be appraised and criticized. Similarly, Goldstein, despite his criticism of oligarchical control in the Transport and General Workers Union argued that there is "no justification for concluding that in such a mass organisation government by oligarchy is inevitable".[60] He argued that "in general, the apathetic rank and file member is an alert and inquisitive person",[61] and if branch life is made more stimulating and exciting then a transformation could take place. "What is lacking", he says, "is that tradition of democracy which only everyday experience, custom and practice can build within the Union".[62] The building of this tradition may be made easier in the future "as the ranks of the Union are filled by working men, who, for the first time in Great Britain's history, will have had schooling till the age of 15 or 16 and have been given the opportunity not only to think but also to enjoy the leisure which thoughtful reflection requires".[63]

This final note of optimism of Lipset et al and Goldstein has not only been echoed by other writers, but in recent years has also be n extended considerably. Some have argued that both Lipset et al and Goldstein, despite traces of optimism, followed Michels too closely and failed to appreciate the number of exceptions to Michels' rule.

Limited Optimism

One writer whose work suggests that there are more exceptions to Michels' rule than some have recognised is Turner.[64] He argued that by no means all British unions are dominated by oligarchies. He suggested that there are three different styles of union government. The first is what he termed the "executive democracy"; this type comes closest to the concept of primitive democracy for the unions are characterised by high membership participation, few full time officials and little distinction between membership and leaders. Such a style of government is typical, Turner argued, of "closed" occupational unions, which have rigid membership controls. The second category was termed the "aristocracies". In these unions the officials are still subject to close scrutiny but by one section rather than by the whole of the membership. This situation is typical, for example, of closed craft unions who have expanded their membership recently; the craft section may retain the right and ability to control the leadership but this privilege may not extend to all sections of the union. The third category is that of "popular bossdoms"; they are characterised by a low level of membership participation and by the greatest difference between the members and the professional officials on which they depend. In such cases senior officials will operate more or less free from control by the bulk of the membership and in effect will be able to appoint their own successors. This style of government is typical of open unions, covering a wide range of occupations.

Using this typology only the third category of unions would bear much resemblance to the kind of oligarchy described by Michels. Unions in the other categories would possess membership or sections of membership with sufficient interest and knowledge to enable them to challenge and control the leadership. It is interesting to note that, taking the case studies by themselves, and leaving out the interpretation and comments of Lipset et al and Goldstein, it would be possible to fit the studies of the ITU and the Transport and General Workers Union into Turner's scheme. The ITU presumably would be placed in the first category of unions; thus, both Lipset et al and Turner would accept that the union was essentially democratic. The Transport and General Workers Union presumably would be placed in the third category; thus, both Goldstein and Turner would accept oligarchical tendencies. However, if the reasoning of the different authors were taken into account then the disagreements between them would be clear; for example, Lipset et al believed that democracy in the ITU was primarily the result of organised opposition whereas Turner saw unions of this type as democratic because of their "closed" nature and the fact that there is little distinction between members and officials or leaders.

Undy and Martin[65] have looked at the extent to which there have been well established opposition groups, and the reasons for them, in British unions. They argue that there have been both opposition and government groups competing for national office over a period of years in a number of British unions. They include, for example, the AUEW(E), CPSA, POEU, EETPU and Equity within that category.

> The group in the AUEW(E) clearly has the features associated with a party and it is probable that the Block in the POEU and the Moderate Group in the CPSA also come into this category. The broad left groups in these latter three unions follow a similar pattern. Indeed they all at different times have held majority control over all or parts of their respective national governing bodies, for example, conference or executive. In contrast, the broad left in the EEPTU has never seriously challenged the moderates' control of the union after the ballot rigging scandal of the late 1950s. Nevertheless, the broad left regrouped and, in the 1980s, despite the fierce antagonism of the established leadership, continued to contest major national elections, with some minor

success.   Equity, in contrast has had a multiplicity of groups challenging the moderate Act for Equity governing group.   The Centre Forward group has probably been the most influential of the opposition groups, and in the early 1980s made a number of gains on Equity's executive.   A further and important feature of all groups in this category is that they publish their own newspapers and/or election addresses and are generally successful in the more important elections in informing the wider membership of the political choice offered by their own candidates.   They therefore reduce "randomness" in elections whilst helping to promote close contests, in some instances defeating incumbents and overturning the established leadership.[66]

Undy and Martin also pointed out that certain membership traits distinguished those unions that had developed government and opposition groups from those that had not.   These features included occupational homogeny and the stability of the historically dominant groups.

Other writers have centred their criticism of the Michels thesis, and the Lipset et al and Goldstein interpretations, not on the number of exceptions to the rule but on the extent to which the mechanisms outlined were described erroneously.   In particular there is a belief that the leaders are subject to challenge at all levels more frequently than some writers have recognised.

Edelstein, in a number of publications,[67] has examined the competition for top union posts. He notes the during "the past few years the presidents of several American unions have been defeated" and that in many British unions close elections are by no means unknown.   He concludes that in both America and Britain "opposition in important elections has been found to be more frequent and more successful than many observers would have thought possible in trade unions".[68]   Undy and Martin[69] in their study of British unions point out that 98 of the 103 unions they surveyed had lay executives and in 93 cases there were required to face re-election after a period in office not exceeding three years.   They also argue that lay executives are often subject to quite high rates of turnover; for example, in 1978, 20 out of an executive committee of 35 in the Transport and General Workers Union had less than five years membership of that committee.   Chaison and Rose[70] make a similar point when they note that turnover amongst union presidents in the United States has been relatively high in recent years; between 1955 and 1971 turnover averaged 21%; while it is recognised that normally turnover is the result of resignation, retirement or failure to seek re-election rather than defeat, it was argued that seemingly voluntary turnover may hide the fact that opposition to an incumbent may be effective in persuading the incumbent not to seek re-election. Edlestein is also supported in his view by writers like Barbash.[71]   He notes that not only have national union presidents and their chosen replacements been defeated in elections, but also that they have been shaken by widespread protests and secessions and negotiated settlements have been defeated by the rank and file.   Wootton's study of the Association of Engineering and Shipbuilding Draftsmen[72] (now part of the AUEW) similarly gives some support to this view by suggesting that the existence of factions in the union meant that elections were more likely to be openly contested and members were likely to be offered a genuine choice.   A rather different note of caution of the interpretation of leadership studies is offered by Strauss when he points out that many of the studies of union leaders were conducted on a particular generation of leaders, and it is at least worthwhile examining whether the new generation behave in similar or different ways to their predecessors.

Flanders has noted the way in which the union convention or conference can be used to control leaders and officials.

The constitutional checks on bureaucracy in the British trade unions are, however, relatively strong. Most of them have annual delegate conferences or the equivalent at which the broad lines of union policy are discussed and decided, in unfettered debate. The passing of resolutions contrary to the executive's recommendations is not an infrequent occurrence.[73]

A similar conclusion was reached by Clegg after a detailed study of the General and Municipal Workers' Union. He argued that "organs of popular control exist and are used. Congress has defeated the platform; and a district secretary has been dismissed by his district council".[74] He added that instances "of this kind are to be found mainly in recent years, which seems to reveal ... that the machinery of democracy within the union ... is not rusting for lack of use, but used more than ever before".[75] More recent evidence can be presented to support this view. For example, although in the Transport and General Workers Unions the platform is rarely defeated at conferences, this is not always the case. Jack Jones, for instance, when General Secretary, was defeated in 1977 on the issue of the Social Contract.

Other writers have noted the way in which regional and local machinery and factions can provide an alternative power base to the national executive. One writer, Martin,[76] is particularly associated with discussion of this last development. He argues that the survival of faction (rather then the survival of opposition, as suggested by Lipset et al) is the best safeguard of democracy in unions. He goes on to list a number of the circumstances likely to lead to the survival of faction; interestingly there are a number of overlaps between his list and one produced from the work of Lipset et al though Dickenson argues that there are fundamental differences between the idea of faction and an opposition party (differences which she claims many writers, including Martin, did not bring out fully). It is worthwhile noting that this view is challenged by Undy and Martin[77] who view factions and parties as opposite ends of a continuum. Support for Martins's thesis can be gained from the work of Nicholas.[78] The importance of factionalism at branch level was highlighted by Nicholson, Ursell and Blyton.[79] They pointed to major changes to the structure of factions during the course of their study and to the way in which on occasions factions sought to influence not just the formulation of policy but alter the implementation.

Other writers have referred to the challenge from the workshop and how this can be seen as a limitation on the power of national leaders. Undy's study of the elections in the Engineering section of the AUEW between 1960 and 1975[80] provides another twist to this debate. He argues that, contrary to the views expressed by Edelstein[81] and Edelstein and Warner,[82] there is evidence of the existence of an effective opposition party within the union which managed to obtain considerable electoral success over a period (including for example the election of Hugh Scanlon as President), but that this party managed to exist without the existence of the conditions that Lipset et al claimed were essential if an opposition party were to be able to operate and without some of the constraints that Martin listed as assisting the survival of faction (such as high level of membership participation and a non-ideological opposition). Undy's explanation is that the opposition party managed to operate because of a number of constraints, inherent within the Union, against extinction by the established leadership. Thus, he said:

Crucially, in the Engineers, the major constraint protecting the opposition is, paradoxically, the leadership's own dependence on a similar unofficial electoral organisation. This dependence is created by the internal structure of the Union which demands that electoral pacts are formed in order to win and retain full-time officers positions of national importance. The repeated and constitutionally prescribed first and second ballot electoral process attracts large numbers of candidates, and puts

13

pressure on like-minded ambitious members, in this case, ideologically like-minded, to combine unofficially to win elections. Thus the established leadership is unwilling to remove the opposition by rule-change or strict enforcement of the rules because to do so would weaken or destroy its own more successful, unofficial organisation. Only when its success is challenged does the establishment seek to alter the electoral system and then it only marginally adjusts it by, for instance, introducing postal ballots.[83]

McCarthy and Parker, in a survey conducted for the Donovan Commission,[84] noted the crucial role of shop stewards in workplace relations.

40% of union members get their information about what is happening in the union from their steward. Slightly more members get such information from their union journal, but when it is borne in mind that 54% of the members who see a union journal get it from their steward, the steward is clearly the main source of keeping the member informed.[85]

This crucial role in communications enables the shop steward to build an effective power base. Cyriax and Oakeshott[86] referred to the way in which shop stewards at Briggs Motor Bodies factory at Dagneham were able to use their position to build a power base which rivalled the official union structure. Davis[87] argued that in the Australian Metal Workers Union the increasing importance of the shop steward system was helping to offset the reduction in membership participation resulting from the decreasing attendances at branch meetings. The power of shop stewards has been referred to by other writers in a wide range of other studies.[88]

Banks[89] uses evidence such as this to suggest that trade unions are governed and policy is made not by oligarchies but by polyarchies. Union leaders, Banks argues, are regularly challenged at all levels by the members. This does not mean that all members take an active part in all union affairs all the time; however, it does mean that union leaders are subject to checks by active union members and cannot merely wield power as they wish. Commenting specifically on the work of Lipset et al, Banks says that what they

failed to appreciate is that representative democracy works on the principle that between the rank and file member and the top men there are very many aspiring leaders whose challenge must be met and whose political skills are not negligible. A proper study of the mechanisms of representative democracy must include an investigation of the part played by district, regional and national assemblies in the development of such skills amongst the erstwhile rank and file.[90]

Banks also argues that many studies of union democracy have concentrated too much on purely structural factors. He suggests that much more attention needs to be given to the motivation of members to take part in union government. Thus, he says; "The study of participation ... can ill afford to ignore the effect of personality and other differences in people and their circumstances which influence the likelihood of their filling participatory roles". A democratic system of union government is one in which "institutional barriers that might prevent members from participating or expressing their opinion have been eliminated. It is not one which results in all the members in the system having the same or equal motives for so behaving".[91]

Banks receives support on this latter issue from Child, Loveridge and Warner[92] when they argue that in the past too much attention has been focused upon characteristics of the union itself in discussions of democracy. They suggest that considerably more attention could be focused on the union member and membership needs (they also draw attention to the importance of the work group as a major reference point for workshop behaviour, the formation of union attachment and the formulation of membership needs).[93] Anderson's work[94] on local municipal unions in Canada also gives some support to Bank's point of view. In his discussion of participation in branch meetings, Anderson points out that participation is not purely dependent on the union structure but also on the individual union member. "The decision to attend a local meeting is, after all, an individual one; although the type of union structure may hinder the ability of members to influence the decision making process, it does not preclude their attendance".[95] A similar point was made by Glick, Mirvis and Harder[96] after their study of a professional engineering union. They argued that participation in union affairs was related more to the characteristics of the individual than anything else; only those individuals "with strong needs for decision making, accomplishment and growth"[97] showed a desire to participate in union affairs, and linked their satisfaction with the union to the extent of their participation. Fosh[98] in her study of Sheffield steelworkers, emphasised intrinsic commitment to trade unionism as a crucial element in determining participation in union affairs while Nicholson, Ursell and Blyton[99] drew attention to the social needs for involvement. In explaining the need for involvement this latter group of authors drew attention to the importance of political socialisation with parental values and educational induction providing the means for individuals to gain beliefs and values about their relations with their union. On a more general level, Banks' views are also echoed in the work of Silverman.[100]

The discussion of trade unions as polyarchies has been taken up by James.[101] He supports Bank's view that trade unions are better seen as polyarchies, rather than oligarchies or democracies, because he believes that the dichotomy between leadership and rank and file is no longer tenable; in trade unions, he says, activists are distributed throughout the union hierarchy and a leadership of sorts is present at a range of different levels within the union. However, he also suggests that while Bank's view is acceptable at a fairly general level, it should be borne in mind that trade unions differ considerably in their forms of government and thus in the scope which they allow active participants to exercise some control over union activities.[102]

However, in many ways the most radical attack on the theory of oligarchy in trade unions has appeared from another direction; it has been linked to the view that an analysis of trade union policy should be based not on the way it impinges on the policy making process, but on the extent to which trade union policy is framed in accordance with the wishes of union members and is effective. Such a viewpoint is possibly most closely associated with the work of Allen.[103]

A Different Definition of Democracy

Allen began by attacking the interpretation of union democracy adopted by most earlier writers. They had viewed union democracy, he said, as analogous to state democracy.[104] As a result they had been concerned to examine the internal mechanisms of government, the rights of individuals and so on. When one is considering state democracy it is quite reasonable to look at such matters. The state, he said, is a compulsory society:

> ... the government is responsible for the maintenance of law and order in society ... One must pay taxes, respect property rights, conform to certain health standards, and do nothing that is obviously injurious to other members of the community. One must obey the judicial interpretations of Parliamentary legislation. It is important, then,

that a mechanism should be provided to enable those who are affected by legislation to have a say in its determination. Further, because one cannot be sure, at any time, that the legislative and administrative organs of a compulsory society can be kept free from manipulation by private interests, there must be some form of popular control.[105]

However, a trade union is not analogous to a state; it is a voluntary not a compulsory society. Consequently it is inappropriate to look at internal mechanisms as a guide to democracy. Such mechanisms are only important when a person cannot leave the society concerned; they are unimportant when people can leave if they disagree with the policy or administration of the society.

Allen does not argue that internal democratic mechanisms have no place within voluntary organisations.[106] He states that the "greater the degree of "member participation" the more virile the organisation is likely to be" and that activity in voluntary societies should be "the beginning of training in social responsibility". Further such activity enables "members to lead a full life, for a man is unable to express himself satisfactorily "by the negative process of contriving an environment where few demands are made of him and where he lives detached from the ordinary preoccupations and concerns of his fellows". However, while such internal democratic mechanisms are desirable, they are not, according to Allen, indispensable. "It is the voluntary nature of organizations within a state which is essential for the preservation of democracy within these organizations".[107]

A trade union is an organisation with a very specific aim. Its aim, Allen believes, can succinctly be stated as "to protect and improve the general living standards of its members".[108] It must be judged by the degree to which it achieves this aim. This means that efficiency is as much a prime concern of a trade union as it is of a business organisation.[109] Trade union leaders, Allen argues, like business leaders, have found that efficiency depends on two factors; first, an essentially bureaucratic organisation and, second, size. "Far from administrative problems being caused by bigness they are reduced by it. The advantages arising out of specialization of labour apply as much to the field of administration as to the field of technology".[110]

If trade unions pursue the interests of their members efficiently then they will, according to Allen, be helping to preserve and extend democracy in society. Unions can persuade management to accept the right of workers to combine in an industry or to have a greater say in industrial decisions; in so doing they will be extending democracy. Voluntary societies in general, by representing members' interests, will be helping to extend democracy in a state.

Allen does not argue that union leaders should be free to use power as they wish. "The use of arbitrary power in trade unions would be inconsistent with the aims of trade unionism and could only result in a violation of those aims. Trade unions are a part of the movement towards real state democracy and they can be an effective part of the movement only by using methods not radically inconsistent with democracy".[111] But how can the power of officials be checked (it is recognised that it is also important for these officials to be able to exercise authority to ensure that the aims of the organisation are efficiently achieved)? This cannot be done by the use of internal mechanisms, for even if they were desirable they would not work.

When there is an inherent tendency in organizations for control to be vested in the hands of a few individuals it is no safeguard against abuse of authority simply to install democratic checks. For various reasons these checks may not be operative. In all organizations, even the state, democratic checks operate only in so far as the leaders and the rank and file want them to operate.[112]

There is, Allen states, only one way of solving this problem and that is by retaining the voluntary character of trade unions.

So long as trade union members have the right to "contract out" of membership if they are dissatisfied with the union they belong to, then a continuous impulse will operate to impel trade-union leaders to retain them. Obviously in a free organization of this nature workers would retain their membership only if they were satisfied with the work the organization was doing. Dissatisfaction would be reflected in a declining membership, and in the interests of self-preservation union leaders would be compelled to stem the tide. They would have to get a correct impression of the needs of workers. The democratic mechanism would be operated from the top.[113]

However, it is not only through declining membership that union leaders can be forced to ensure that they are in step with the rank and file; it is also the fear that in the future if they take the wrong action, membership may decline. "Always, therefore, leadership must walk in step with the rank and file".[114]

One interesting sidelight on Allen's thesis is that it has led him to oppose compulsory unionism, in particular the "closed shop". "Compulsory trade unionism" he says "would remove from workers that right to move freely within the context of the democratic state which is a measure of democracy. It would also remove the one check on the authority of trade union leaders which operates automatically and which ensures that the democratic mechanism in trade unionism is used to the best advantage".115

A number of writers have supported Allen's contention that it is erroneous to apply the model of state democracy to trade unions. For example, Hughes has argued that "trade union government involves an electoral situation and underlying social relations simpler than, and in some ways significantly different from, those of our political democracy". He concludes that "trade union democracy cannot be analysed simply by analogy from, or in terms of the accepted norms of, the political democracy of nation states".[116] Some support can also be seen in the work of McGrath[117] who argues that the problems of union government cannot be dealt with by looking in the traditional way at union democracy. Democracy of this kind, he feels, is inappropriate and impossible to achieve in organisations like trade unions. Support can also be gained from the work of Bealey.[118] In his study of the Post Office Engineering Union he argues that it is wrong to equate democracy in a trade union with democracy in a state. If trade union members have to choose between democratic mechanisms and the efficient operation of their union, then they are likely to choose the latter rather than the former. "This is because the salient and pressing goal of the trade union, getting more money for members is largely pre-determined by its raison d'etre. Within the democratic state, on the other hand, goals are not usually postulated and are therefore open to dispute".[119] He concludes his study of the Post Office Engineering Union by arguing that members were concerned that the union should be efficient enough to fight a "monolithic" employer and should avoid the damaging internal splits of the past. This meant that they were willing to allow policy primarily to be made by a professional bureaucracy with the General Secretary at its head. Thus he said; "If "democracy" entails a leadership operating within a framework of consent by the led, the POEW is "democratic" in spite of being "oligarchic". How undemocratic is it to decide freely to be led by an oligarchy".[120] Urwin and Murray[121] take up the issue of the voluntary nature of trade unions raised by Allen and give some support to his argument by suggesting that participation "acts as a profoundly practical constraint on both trade union leaders and activists". They go on to argue that the

charge that unions are in general unrepresentative of their members should be treated sceptically since they are in fact uniquely reliant on the voluntary and active participation of their members for the organization of their affairs and the pursuit of their objectives. ... Both shop stewards and officials depend on their ability to persuade their members in favour of a course of action. Their judgement about what course of action to recommend is often complex and must be finely tuned to the feelings of the broad mass of members.[122]

More generally there is an argument that concentration on particular mechanisms associated with democracy is misleading. For example, concentration on the number of people voting in elections implies that a high percentage poll is an indication of a democratic organisation, when, in practice, so that argument goes, this may be far from the case. Bray and Davis[123] recall the debate about the percentage turnout in the Presidential election for the Australian Metal Workers Shipwrights Union and how the left argued that turnout was no guide to the extent of democracy in the union.

Democracy is a continuing process not just a single act of placing a piece of paper in a ballot box every few years. Above all democracy means participation ... those people who imagine that they can exercise their democratic rights by occasionally casting a secret vote are deluding themselves. It is the very opposite of democracy - which is government by the people, not government of the people by few.[124]

However, Allen's thesis has also attracted a good deal of criticism. This can be narrowed down to four main areas of contention. First, a number of authors have argued that Allen's basic premise is incorrect; trade unions are not voluntary associations. Thus Lipset says; "The principle premise, in the argument that oligarchic unions may be regarded as democratic, rests, as Allen makes clear, on the assumption that trade unions are voluntary associations which members may leave much as they may quit a stamp club when they object to what it is doing". However, he argues that this "assumption clearly does not apply to most American trade unions ... Under the closed shop, and more recently the union shop, men cannot legally quit their union without losing their jobs".[125] Even where the member has the legal power to leave a union and keep a job this is relatively meaningless because the union can blacklist the ex-member and deprive him of substantial pension rights and the like. In a similar vein Hall[126] has pointed out how the provisions of the Taft-Hartley Act have been used to strengthen an American union's hold over reluctant members. The Act makes it difficult for dissident members to leave a union and join another, or to establish another, because of the provisions on bargaining rights.[127] Similar comments have been made about the position in Britain. Flanders[128] referred to McCarthy's[129] estimate that about 3 million trade unionists in Britain work in a closed shop and argued that this meant that "unions are assured of their (members) support regardless of their policies and activities".[130] More recent examination of the extent of the closed shop in Britain by Gennard[131] and through the Workplace Industrial Relations Survey[132] has suggested that between 18% and 27% of all employees are covered by it with the proportion amongst manual workers being considerably higher (the 1984 Workplace Industrial Relations Survey suggested that 30% of all manual workers were covered by the closed shop).

The second criticism has centred on the inability of members to challenge or even evaluate official policy because of their lack of knowledge or the lack of open debate. Thus Slichter has argued that the "great majority of the members do not have much opportunity or desire to consider and discuss alternative policies". Hence they are not to be regarded as making a choice.[133] Similarly, Cyriax and Oakeshott have noted that even in union elections, "there is rarely a real clash of wills and choice of candidates which would bring out the issues at stake".[134]   As a result, union members may stay in a union not because they agree with the policies being followed or because they accept that the union is being run efficiently but simply because they have no way of finding out about such matters.

This issue is taken a stage further by Moran[135] who argues that most union members have little or no interest in the affairs of their union.   Continued membership is merely an indication of apathy, not contentment or agreement.   This is particularly true of certain aspects of union activity and aims.   Most unions in Britain and in Western Europe (if not in the U.S.A.) have political (specifically socialist) aspirations and a considerable amount of effort is directed to this area.   Many union members show little real sympathy for such aims or activity (this is confirmed broadly in Goldthorpe and Lockwood's study[136]): however, they do no react against it, they are merely apathetic towards it.   Moran's point has some similarities with the finding of Rose[137] that a union member may be highly loyal to his union, yet remain critical of many aspects of its work.

The third line of criticism concerns the extent to which membership figures can be seen as a good guide to membership satisfaction.   Allen, of course, is not alone in arguing that membership figures are a useful measure of membership interest and approval; they were used in a similar fashion by Goldstein in his study of the Transport and General Workers' Union.[138]   However, their use in such a way has been challenged by a number of writers. Hughes[139] uses a survey of lapsed membership in the Union of Shop Distributive and Allied Workers to show that only a small proportion of members left because they were dissatisfied with the union or because of apathy; thus, whereas 85% left the union because they either gave up employment or took up employment in another trade, only 1.6% left because they were dissatisfied with the union. Eldridge makes a similar point. He says: " ... membership fluctuations can only in a very guarded sense be treated as an indicator of membership satisfaction or dissatisfaction. The fluctuations may be caused by quite other factors, such as the general level of employment and the particular fortunes of the industries in which the union operates".[140]

The fourth line of criticism centres on the notion that unions have well defined aims; in particular, that they have aims and objectives subscribed to by all members and officers. There are a vast number of studies which show that such an assumption is difficult to support. For example, Kendall[141] has argued that although in Europe many union leaders see the organisation as having a primarily political role, most members view their association in a purely instrumental light.   It is also clear in Britain that although some union activists place emphasis on the political role, other groups do not.   Clegg, Killick and Adams[142] noted that union officials gave low priority to political objectives even though they were given high priority by the union rule books.   Howells and Woodfield in their survey of workers' preferences in New Zealand[143] record the insensitivity of union officers to members' aims and objectives.

At first sight these criticisms appear damning and they certainly have led most writers to reject Allen's thesis in its present form.   However, at the same time, many of the writers who reject Allen's thesis as outlined appear to accept a modification of it.   A thesis which stated that union leaders will react to and modify policy in the face of criticism from their members (which may be expressed in a variety of different forms, such as strike action, membership lapses, the establishment of rival unions) seems to be accepted by most commentators. Clearly this differs from Allen's original formulation: it says nothing about the ability of members to criticise, or their ability to leave a union.

Many writers, as has been seen above, would argue that union members are unlikely to be able to criticise union policy or leave a union as a form of protest.   What this hypothesis suggests, however, is that on occasions members may protest, and that if they do so, union leaders will be compelled to take note.   It should also be stated that most writers would probably argue that the conditions outlined above are insufficient to enable one to talk about union democracy, but if one is interested in policy making rather than attaching labels, then this may not matter.

The classic example, often quoted, of a situation in which a union leader was forced to alter the policy he pursued because of the reaction of union members concerns John L Lewis of the United Mineworkers of America. Lewis became President of the Mineworkers union in 1919 after the then President, Hayes, had been forced to resign. Initially Lewis assumed the post on a temporary basis but this was converted to a permanent position in an election held the following year. Lewis thus assumed control of "the largest, the richest, and by far the most powerful union in America".[144] The first twelve years of Lewis's reign as President, however, were disastrous. He adopted a conservative stance; Finley says that prior to 1933 he "was regularly called one of the most reactionary men in American labour, with no program, no vision, no concept of the future".[145] The U.S.A. mining industry, like that in other countries, suffered considerably during this period. Lewis's plan was to allow economic forces to work themselves out. He put forward his programme for the industry in 1923: "Shut down 4,000 coal mines, force 200,000 miners into other industries and the coal problem will settle itself ... it is better to have half a million men working in the industry at good wages ... than to have a million working in poverty".[146] Throughout the 1920s Lewis took no action either to halt the closures in the industry or to re-capture lost union members. By the early 1930s disillusionment in the union had reached such a state that two major attempts were made to form breakaway unions. The second of these attempts led to the establishment of the Progressive Miners of America Union, a body which survived to provide a constant, if less than spectacular, example of the dissension in the miners' ranks.

By 1932 membership of the union had fallen to something between 60,000 and 100,000; when Lewis became President of the union it had stood at half a million. The union was no longer able to bargain effectively on behalf of its members or enforce contracts made. Finley comments that:

> If John L Lewis had departed the labour movement in 1933, or had met an untimely death, those scholars of labour's past would indeed have placed a harsh judgement upon him. His years in office to that point had been filled with the almost virtual destruction of the United Mineworkers of America. It had lost its contracts, its wage scales, its membership. Its once great treasury, the pride of America's unions, was thin and insecure. It had no strength to resist the operators, who could even count on the support of Lewis himself when they needed it.[147]

The decline in membership and the attempts to form breakaway unions apparently persuaded Lewis to change course dramatically. Almost overnight he changed from being one of the most conservative to become one of the most militant union leaders. "The stricken union arose. It revived. The feat was accomplished in a few hectic months, as in blitz times when wars are won".[148] In 1933 the leaders of the union initiated and supported a successful series of strikes for wage increases. The contract negotiated as a settlement following strikes in the Appalachian coalfield covered a wide range of issues from the check-off to the eight hour day and has been called "the greatest in magnitude and scope" ever negotiated in the United States".[149] The members came flocking back to the union. "Enthusiasm was so high that miners were sworn into membership by mass inductions ... Organizers who had not signed a new member in years were deluged with requests to join the new army. They told each other in amazement, "By God, the old union is coming back."[150]

The case of Lewis was cited by Lipset[151] when he accepted the notion that union leaders in a general sense must be responsive to the demands of their members. Thus Lipset et al said:

"A union oligarchy which does not defend the economic interests of the rank and file may find its membership disappearing either into another union or into nonmembership in any union, as John L Lewis did in the twenties and early thirties". Lewis, then a trade union as well as a political conservative, almost lost the United Mine Workers. Only after adopting the militant tactics for which he is now famous was he able to rebuild the union. "A trade union which is not an economic defense organization has no function and will not long remain on the scene".[152] Lipset makes it clear that he feels that this does not negate his or Michels' thesis. Thus he states that to recognise that a union must be responsible to demands made by members or signs of dissatisfaction "does not involve declaring that a trade union is necessarily representative of its members' interests or must be considered a democratic organization".[153] Often members will simply not express an opinion openly or forcefully or not be able to do so. Nevertheless, Lipset makes it clear that if members do express an opinion forcefully then the leadership cannot ignore it.

This general point seems to be accepted by Warner.[154] He argues that even in a large union, where the closed shop is in operation the "membership must be kept minimally happy, and never taken for granted". If there is widespread dissatisfaction the union rank and file must be satisfied. "Otherwise membership will drop and the power of the un on and of its leaders will drop with it".[155]

Again, Fox argues, that there "is still the minimum of service which leaders must render to members' goals if they are to retain their authority. Cases are numerous", he says, "where in the absence of the minimum, members have withdrawn legitimacy and vested it in the unofficial leaders of lower level collectivities. Grass roots power born of labour scarcity has greatly enhanced their power to do so, younger and more militant aspirants to office will not be slow to make use of the fact".[156]

Wright-Mills[157] makes a similar point in general terms. He clearly believes that union leaders have a great deal of power over their members and members are often in no position to judge the action of the leaders; much of the activity of the leadership is hidden from view. However leaders have to react to changing economic conditions and the demands of the membership. If they do not, then they are likely to be overthrown. Thus he states: "During slumps especially when the rank and file are militant, leaders of labour must shift to more militant ways or gamble on losing their leadership".[158]

Many union leaders themselves have echoed the claim of academics that to a certain extent they must be seen by their members to be "delivering the goods". Possibly the most flamboyant statement of this kind has come from Hoffa, the President of the American Teamsters' Union. "Most people do not want to participate in the day-to-day operations of their union - this is the business agent's job. But when people are really dissatisfied or hurt, watch out for the fireworks. A leader must deliver what the people really want".[159]

Moran, after his study of the Union of Post Office Workers,[160] argued that one should not be misled because of the apathy of union members on some issues (such as socialist aspirations) into believing that union members are likely to be apathetic on all issues. There are certain issues, mainly concerning the terms and conditions of employment about which the union member is keenly concerned. If the union leaders adopt a policy on these issues contrary to the wishes of the membership then there is likely to be a backlash. Moran gave one instance of an attempt by the leaders of the Post Office Workers Union in the 1920s to impose a policy to which the majority of members seemed to object. The policy involved the setting up of a strike fund and a levy to support that fund. The bulk of the membership, Moran argues, opposed those moves, and were particularly incensed by the levy. As a result, the union lost over half its membership.

The revised Allen thesis almost ironically also seems to be compatible with Michels' iron law of oligarchy. One of the central themes of Michels' argument is that union leaders are concerned to protect their own position. This normally means that they act in a conservative fashion. However, if they were faced with a challenge to their position, on the basis of the Michels' thesis, one would not expect them to stand by some policy on principle. If the challenge was genuine then the likely outcome, following the Michels thesis, surely would be for them to change their policy to protect this position. Michels did not pay a great deal of attention to such developments because he believed that expressions of membership discontent were unlikely; however, as has been noted, subsequent writers have argued that although expressions of membership discontent are unlikely they are nevertheless perfectly possible and on occasion do occur.

It is important to stress, though, that the revised thesis is a very general one indeed. It does not state exactly how many members must express discontent before leaders need to take notice, or exactly what kind of action leaders must take to placate disgruntled members. Most writers would suggest that an attempt to set up a breakaway union would seem as an important event and one which leaders could not ignore. Lerner[161], for example, in her study of breakaway unions, shows that leaders of the National Union of Tailors and Garment Workers and the Post Office Engineering Union responded to attempts by groups to secede by modifying their stance on a number of issues: in the former case, the leadership reorganised the administrative structure and adopted a different personal style, while in the latter case the leaders attempted to make some moves to decentralise the union. However, Lerner recognises that leaders can respond in a number of different ways and that they may feel that they have to take note of the need to maintain a viable organisation. Thus, she says:

> The full-time leaders who make the day to day decisions of the union tend to identify their own decisions with those of the union as a whole. They develop a sense of responsibility towards the employers' associations to observe the agreement. They reason that if agreements were not observed, collective bargaining would collapse. Since the National Executive Council or some other representative body had approved the agreement, the union must honour it. The leaders are concerned with the maintenance of the union as a powerful institution, with the processing of grievances through accepted channels, and with respecting the unions's rules.[162]

It may be, then, the union leaders will have to weigh up whether a move to placate disgruntled members might do more harm than good to the union as a whole; if, for example, it might weaken the union or the union leaders' ability to bargain with employers.

The point concerning the competing pressures on union leaders is dealt with by Hemingway in his study of disputes in three trade unions.[163] Recalling the dispute in the Bridgend busman's branch of the National Union of Railwaymen, Hemingway argues that more was at stake than the particular issues under discussion. "It was abundantly clear that what was at stake was the question of who was going to exercise control over union policy".[164] If the union leaders had conceded over the issues being debated, then their concessions could have had widespread repercussions. In one of the other case studies, that of the insurance agents, Hemingway notes that union leaders had to recognise that the breakaway group represented a minority and that if they made moves to satisfy minority interests, they might run the risk of antagonising the majority. Hemingway does not suggest that any particular outcome will necessarily result from a dispute between leaders and members, even if the dispute involves secession on the part of a group of members. Rather he argues that disputes between union leaders and members should be seen as part of a process of bargaining. "At any point in the bargaining process, therefore, one side may win a victory or both may compromise. The parties might alternatively expend all their resources and strategic options and reach a stalemate, with the conflict perhaps falling into abeyance".[165]

Child, Loveridge and Warner[166] raise the related issue of the leadership's interpretation of members' representations. Linking this to a leader's sense of proprietorship towards different categories of membership, the term proprietorship is used to indicate that a union leader may view different sections of the union's membership ways, seeing some of them as central but others as more peripheral.

There is, then much still to be explored. While many writers would acknowledge that union leaders must take notice of vocal opposition to policies by members, particularly if that opposition takes the form or members leaving a union, there is no clear statement on the extent of such opposition that is necessary before action will be taken and there is no clear view on what kind of action leaders must take. It may be action to placate the disgruntled members, to meet their demands, or it may be action to try to isolate them and ensure that the dispute affects the rest of the union as little as possible.

Notes

1. Their books, S & B Webb, *A History of Trade Unionism*, Longmans, London, 1896 and S & B Webb, *Industrial Democracy*, Longmans, Green & Co., London, 1920 have been given the status of industrial relations "classics".
    V L Allen in *The Sociology of Industrial Relations*, Longmans, London 1971 says "There was in a sense, no trade union history until they (the Webbs) wrote it" (p28) while G S Bain and H A Clegg in "A Strategy for Industrial Relation Research in Great Britain", British Journal of Industrial Relations, Vol.XII, No.1, March 1974 refer to *Industrial Democracy* as industrial relations', "major and perhaps only classic", (p98).
2. S & B Webb, 1920, *Op Cit*, pp3-4.
3. *Ibid,* p8.
4. The vast majority of trade unions in Britain were still fairly small when compared to current standards. No union approached the two million members recently claimed by Britain's largest union, the Transport and General Workers Union. A number of writers have argued that the problems of democracy in trade unions are linked to size; see, for example, M Warner, L Donaldson, "Dimensions of Organization in Occupational Interest Association; Some Preliminary Findings", Third Joint Conference on Behavioural Science and Operational Research, London, 1971, who looked, in particular, at the ability of members to control officers in unions of differing size.
5. S & B Webb, 1920, *Op Cit*, p8.
6. *Ibid*, pp36-7.
7. *Ibid*, p41.
8. It is worthwhile noting that very few British unions have, in fact, adopted the Webbs' model of representative democracy machinery.
9. J E T Eldridge in *Sociology and Industrial Life*, Nelson, London, 1973 implies that the Webbs' conclusion was pessimistic (pp177-8) and states that they came to the same conclusion as Michels. While it is correct to state that the Webbs and Michels looked at the same phenomena and highlighted similar tendencies, it is difficult to view the Webbs' account in such a pessimistic light because they saw a way of overcoming the problems observed whereas Michels did not.
10. R Michels, *Political Parties*, Free Press, New York, 1962.

11. *Ibid*, p16.

12. *Ibid*, p17.

13. *Ibid*, p365.

14. *Ibid*, p353.

15. *Ibid*, p353.

16. *Ibid*, p154.

17. N Bukharin in *Historical Materialism: A System of Sociology*, International Publishers, New York, 1925 recognised that the transition from capitalism to socialism, the period of the "proletarian dictatorship", might present problems and might lead to the emergence of a new leading stratum. See also, P Selznick, *The Organizational Weapon: A Study of Bolshevik Strategy and Tactics*, McGraw-Hill, New York, 1952.

18. Quoted by S M Lipset, in his introduction to R Michels, *Op Cit*, at p26.

19. T Lane, *The Union Makes Us Strong*, Arrow Books, London, 1974, p30.

20. Michels, *Op Cit*, p367.

21. Michels, *Op Cit*, p367.

22. S M Lipset, M A Trow, J S Coleman, *Union Democracy*, Free Press, New York, 1956.

23. *Ibid*, p13.

24. *Ibid*, p413.

25. J Goldstein, *The Government of a British Trade Union*, Free Press, Glencoe, 1952.

26. *Ibid*, p70.

27. *Ibid*, p73.

28. *Ibid*, p113.

29. *Ibid*, p132.

30. *Ibid*, p269.

31. B C Roberts, *Trade Union Government and Administration in Great Britain*, Harvard U.P., Cambridge (Mass), 1956.

32. *Political and Economic Planning*, P.E.P., London, 1948.

33. J H Goldthorpe, D Lockwood, F Bechhofer, J Platt, *The Affluent Worker: Industrial Attitudes and Behaviour*, Cam ridge U.P., London, 1958.

34. W W Daniel, N Milward, *Workplace Industrial Relations in Britain*, Heinemann, London, 1983.

35. See J Seldman, B Karsh, D Tagliacozzo, "A Typology of Rank-and-File Union Members", American Journal of Sociology, Vol 4, 1956, pp546-53 and J Seidman, J London, B Karsh, D Tagliacozzo, *The Workers Views His Union*, University of Chicago Press, Chicago, 1958.

36. R Lumley, *White Collar Unionism in Britain*, Methuen, London, 1973.

37. G D H Cole, *An Introduction to Trade Unionism*, Allen & Unwin, London, 1953.

38. *Op Cit.*

39. E Davis, *Decision Making in the Australian AMWU*, Industrial Relations, Vol 16, No.2, May 1977, pp126-132,

40. G Cyriax, R Oakeshott, *The Bargainers*, Faber, London, 1960, pp74-5.

41. International Labour Office, *The Trade Union Situation in the United Kingdom*, I.L.O., Geneva, 1961.

42. For details of ballots see, M P Jackson, *The Price of Coal*, Croom Helm, London, 1974.

43. W E J McCarthy, S R Porter, *Shop Stewards and Workshop Relations*, Royal Commission on Trade Unions and Employers' Associations, 1965-81, Research Paper 10, HMSO, London, 1968.

44. N Millward, M Stevens, *British Workplace Industrial Relations 1980-1984*, Gower, Aldershot, 1986.

45. L Sayles, G Strauss, *The Local Union*, Harcourt Brace, New York, 1953.

46. A S Tannenbaum, R L Kahn, *Participation in Union Locals*, Row and Peterson, Evanston (Illinois), 1958.

47. C Wright-Mills, *The New Men of Power*, Harcourt Brace, New York, 1948. (1971 reprint by Augustus M Keeley).

48. C Wright-Mills, *The Power Elite*, Oxford U.P., New York, 1959.

49. See also, R A Dahl, *A Critique of the Ruling Elite Model*, American Political Science Review, Vol 52, 1958, pp463-9 for criticism of Wright-Mills thesis.

50. J R Coleman, *The Compulsive Pressures of Union Democracy*, American Journal of Sociology, Vol 61, No.6, 1955, pp519-26.

51. B Hall (ed), *Autocracy and Insurgency in Organized Labour*, Transaction Books, New Brunswick, 1972.

52. B C Roberts, *Trade Unions in a Free Society*, Hutchinson, London, 1962, p125.

53. *Ibid*, p35.

54. G Strauss, *Union Government in the U.S.: Research Past and Future*, Industrial Relations, Vol 16, No.2, May 1977, pp215-42.

55. C Kerr, *Unions and Union Leaders of Their Own Choosing*, The Fund for the Republic, New York, 1957.

56. C Summers, "Union Democracy and Union Discipline", Proceedings of New York Universities Fifth Annual Conference on Labour, Matthew Bander, New York, 1952.

57. W M Leiserson, *American Trade Union Democracy*, Columbia U.P., New York, 1959.

58. L Broomwich, *Union Constitutions*, The Fund for the Republic, New York, 1959.

59. S M Lipset, M A Trow, J S Coleman, *Op Cit*, p412.

60. J Goldstein, *Op Cit*, p271.

61. *Ibid*, p270.

62. *Ibid*, p271.

63. *Ibid*, pp271-2.

64. H A Turner, *Trade Union Growth, Structure and Policy*, Allen & Unwin, London, 1962.

65. R Undy, R Martin, *Ballots and Trade Union Democracies*, Blackwell, Oxford 1982.

66. *Ibid*, p194.

67. See, for example, J D Edelstein, *An Organizational Theory of Union Democracy*, American Sociological Review, Vol 32, 1967, pp19-31.

68. J D Edelstein, M Warner, *Comparative Union Democracy*, Transaction Books, New Brunswick, 1979, p112.

69. *Op cit.*

70. G N Chaison, J B Rose, *Turnover Amongst Presidents of Construction National Unions*, Industrial Relations Journal, Vol 16, No.2, May 1977, pp199-204.

71. J Barbash, *American Unions*, Random House, New York, 1967.

72. G Wootton, *Parties in Union Government: the AESD*, Political Studies, Vol 9, June 1961, pp141-56.

73. A Flanders, *Trade Unions*, Hutchinson, London, 1968, p49.

74. H A Clegg, *General Union*, Blackwell, Oxford, 1954, p344.

75. *Ibid*, p344.

76. R Martin, "Union Democracy: An Explanatory Framework", *Sociology*, Vol 2, 1968, pp205-220.

77. *Op Cit.*

78. A W Nicholas, "Factions: A Comparative Analysis", in A S A Monograph, No.2, *Political Systems and the Distribution of Power*, Tavistock, London, 1965.

79. N Nicholson, G Ursell, P Blyton, *The Dynamics of White Collar Unionism*, Academic Press, London, 1981.

80. R Undy, *The Electoral Influence of the Opposition Party in the AUEW Engineering*

      Section 1960-75, British Journal of Industrial Relations, Vol XVII, No.1, March 1974, pp19-23.

81. J Edelstein, *Democracy in a National Unions The British AEU*, Industrial Relations Journal, Vol 4, No.3.

82. *Op Cit*

83. *Ibid*, p32.

84. W E J McCarthy, S R Parker, *Op Cit.*

85. *Ibid.*

86. G Cyriax, R Oakeshott, *Op Cit*

87. *Op Cit.*

88. See, for example, J F B Goodman, T G Whittingham, *Shop Stewards in British Industry*, McGraw-Hill, London, 1969. For a more recent study of workshop relations, see M G Wilders, S R Parker, *Changes in Workplace Industrial Relations, 1966-72*, British Journal of Industrial Relations, Vol XIII, No.1, 1975, pp14-22.

89. J A Banks, *Trade Unionism*, Collier MacMillan, London, 1974.

90. *Ibid*, p90.

91. *Ibid*, p93.

92. J Child, R Loveridge, M Warner, *Towards an Organisational Study of Trade Unions*, Sociology, Vol 7, 1973, pp71-91.

93. See, W Spinard, *Correlates of Trade Union Participation: A Summary of the Literature*, American Sociological Review, Vol 25, 1960. pp237-44. Spinard reviews a number of other studies of trade union participation and shows how factors such as personal association, the conditions of the job and the extent to which work is a central life interest, have been seen as indicators.

94. J A Anderson, *A Comparative Analysis of Local Union Democracy*, Industrial Relations, Vol 17, No.3, Oct. 1978, pp278-95.

95. *Ibid*, p288.

96. W Glick, P Mirvis, D Harder, *Union Satisfaction and Participation*, Industrial Relations Journal, Vol 16, No.2, May 1977, pp145-151.

97. *Ibid*, p151.

98. P Fosh, *The Active Trade Unionist*, Cambridge University Press, Cambridge, 1981.

99. *Op Cit.*

100. D Silverman, *The Theory of Organisations*, Heinemann, London, 1970.

101. L James, "Sources of Legitimate Power in Polyarchic Trade Union Government", *Sociology*, Vol 15, No.2, May   , pp251-261.

102. *Ibid*, p252.

103. V L Allen, *Power in Trade Unions*, Longmans, Green & Co., London, 1954.

104. Subsequently such a definition was used by S M Lipset, M A Trow, J S Coleman, *Op Cit.* See also, J Steiber, *Governing the U A W*, Wiley, New York, 1967. He argues that democracy is a general phenomenon and there cannot be a special type for trade unions.

105. V L Allen, 1954, *Op Cit*, p10.

106. He also notes that trade unions compare favourably with other voluntary associations in terms of internal democratic procedures.

107. V L Allen, 1954, *Op Cit*, p11.

108. *Ibid*, p15.

109. Allen seems to accept a point stressed by many other writers that there may be some conflict between efficiency and internal democratic procedures. He does not see the conflict as inevitable, but when such conflict occurs, seems to believe that efficiency is of prime importance.

110.   V L Allen, 1954, *Op Cit*, p21.
111.   *Ibid*, p26.
112.   *Ibid*, pp26-7.
113.   *Ibid*, p28.
114.   *Ibid*, p28.
115.   *Ibid*, p59.
116.   J Hughes, *Trade Union Structure and Government*, Research Paper 5, Part 2, Royal Commission on Trade Unions and Employers' Association, 1965-8, HMSO, London, 1968.
117.   C P Magrath, *Democracy in Overalls: The Futile Quest for Union Democracy*, Industrial and Labour Relations Review, Vol 12, 1958-9, pp503-25.
118.   F Bealey, *The Political System of the Post Office Engineering Union*, British Journal of Industrial Relations, Vol 15, No.3, 1977, pp374-395.
119.   *Ibid*, p393.
120.   *Ibid*, p393-4.
121.   H Urwin, C Murray, "Democracy and Trade Unions", *Industrial Relations Journal*, Vol 14, No.4, 1983, pp21-30.
        122.*Ibid*, pp128-9.
123.   M Bray, E Davies, Trade Union Democracy from the Inside: Comparison of the British AUEW and Australian AMWSU, *Industrial Relations Journal*, Vol XIII, No.4, Winter 1982, pp84-93.
124.   *Ibid*, p
125.   S M Lipset, M A Trow, J S Coleman, *Op Cit*, p410.
126.   B Hall (ed), *Op Cit*.
127.   This point of view is challenged by P Taft, "Internal Affairs of Unions and the Taft-Hartley Act", *Industrial and Labour Relations Review*, Vol II, No.3, pp354-355.
128.   A Flanders, *Op Cit*.
129.   W E J McCarthy, *The Closed Shop in Britain*, Blackwell, Oxford, 1964.
130.   A Flanders, *Op Cit*, p44.
131.   S Dunn, J Gennard, *The Closed Shop in British Industry*, MacMillan, London, 1984.
132.   *Op Cit*.
133.   S H Slichter, *Challenge of Industrial Relations*, Cornell U.P., Ithca, 1947.
134.   G Cyriax, R Oakeshott, *Op Cit*. p75.
135.   M Moran, *The Union of Post Office Workers: A Study of Political Sociology*, MacMillan, London, 1974.
136.   J H Goldthorpe, D Lockwood, F Bechhofer, J Platt, *Op Cit*.
137.   A Rose, *Union Solidarity*, University of Minesota Press, Minneapolis, 1952.
138.   J Goldstein, *Op Cit*.
139.   J Hughes, *Op Cit*.
140.   J E T Eldridge, *Op Cit*, p180.
141.   W Kendall, *The Labour Movement in Europe*, Allen Lane, London, 1975.
142.   H A Clegg, A J Killick, R Adams, *Trade Union Officers*, Blackwell, Oxford, 1961.
143.   J M Howells, A E Woodfield, *The Ability of Managers and Trade Union Officers to Predict Workers' Preferences*, British Journal of Industrial Relations, Vol VIII, 1970, pp237-251.
144.   J E Finley, *The Corrupt Kingdom*, Simon and Shuster, New York, 19(2, p48.
145.   *Ibid*, p74.
146.   *Ibid*, p61.
147.   *Ibid*, p73.
148.   *Ibid*, p77.

149. *Ibid*, p83.

150. *Ibid*, p79.

151. In both S M Lipset, M A Trow, J S Coleman, *Op Cit*, and Lipset's introduction to R Michels, *Op Cit*.

152. S M Lipset, M A Trow, J S Coleman, *Op Cit*, p409.

153. *Ibid*, p409.

154. M Warner, *Industrial Conflict Revisited*, in M Warner (ed) *The Sociology of the Workplace*, Allen & Unwin, London, 1973, pp256-73.

155. *Ibid*, p369. See, also, J E T Eldridge, *Op Cit*. Eldridge reviews Allen's work and comments that there is a clear distinction between Allen's assertion that members will leave a union if they disagree with policy and Lipset's acceptance that union leaders will have to take note of expressions of rank and file discontent. However, Eldridge does not challenge Lipset's assertion as such and thus, implicity might be seen as giving some support to the revised Allen thesis.

156. A Fox, *A Sociology of Work in Industry*, Collier-MacMillan, London, 1972, p123.

157. C Wright-Mills, 1948, *Op Cit*.

158. *Ibid*, p106.

159. Quoted by S Romer, *The International Brotherhood of Teamsters*, Wiley, New York, 1967, p142, For a more extensive discussion of Hoffa's leadership see R C James, D E James, *Hoffa and the Teamsters*, D Van Nostrand, Princeton, 1965.

160. M Moran, *Op Cit*.

161. S W Lerner, *Breakaway Unions and the Small Trade Union*, Allen and Unwin, London, 1961.

162. *Ibid*, p190.

163. J Hemingway, *Conflict and Democracy: Studies in Trade Union Government*, Oxford University Press, Oxford, 1978.

164. *Ibid*, p124.

165. *Ibid*, pp24-25.

166. J Child, R Loveridge, M Warner, "Towards an Organisational Study of Trade Unions", *Sociology*, Vol 7, 1973, pp71-91.

2 Early attempts to reform the casual system of employment

Casual Employment

Dock workers traditionally have been casual workers: some writers have used dock work as the classic example of casual employment and the rule by which the casualness of other employment could be measured.[1] As fas as dock work is concrened, at the beginning of the the twentieth century, most of the men engaged on work were hired by the half-day." Dock employers would select the men they needed for each half-day at a "calling-on place", which in practice might be no more than a street corner. The number of "calling-on place" varied from port to port, partly according to the geography of the docks: in London, the way a number of employers selected the men they needed was not entirely random. Frequently they gave preference to certain men who had worked for them before. Such men might manage to gain fairly regular employment for lengthy periods, but even for them, employment was not entirely predictable and certainly was not permanent. Other men who did not have "preference" status had even less predictable employment opportunities. If the were unable to obtain work on the docks then they might attempt to find employment elsewhere for a short while, sometimes in occupations closely related to dock work. In other cases they might simply wait, without any alternative employment, until they found work on the docks. The number of jobs available on the docks at any one time depended on a number of factors. The work of loading and unloading varied, largely according to the number and type of ships using the docks. This number fluctuated widely from day to day (and from half day to half day) according to the season, tide, weather and other factors like the demand for particular goods. It was claimed[3] that these fluctuations were unpredictable and that it was impossible to accurately forecast the future demand for labour, let alone to stabilise such demand.

The result was that in most ports the pool of labour from which dock workers were drawn was usually larger than the average demand for labour: there was a reserve of labour that could be called on when demand was high but which could be dispensed with when demand was low. Further, in many ports the pool of labour was higher than ever the maximum number of workers likely to be needed at any one time. However, this pool was not well defined nor stable. While some men spent most of their working life on the docks, others undertook dock work only intermittently, possibly when work in other industries was slack. As a result it was not easy to define accurately the size of the pool of labour available for dock work at any particular port at a particular time: the best that one might be able to do was to indicate the number of men who had worked on the docks at any time over a particular period, though in many ports even this was not easy because of the large number of employers, some of whom might be casual themselves.

Such a system of employment was recognised as being undesirable by a wide range of people. Many of the social commentators of the late nineteenth and early twentieth centuries highlighted casual employment as a major cause of concern. The Webbs, in their minority report for the Poor Law Commission of 1909, said:

> The existence of a large class of underemployed men living on casual jobs, and habitually unable to get anything like a full week's work is universally recognised to be a great social evil. Their average earnings for the year are so low that even with careful management they are unable to procure for themselves and their families the necessaries of a healthy life. They are the occupants of the overcrowded one and two-roomed homes ... Among them privation and exposure and the insanitary conditions of their dwellings lead to an excessive prevalence of disease of all kinds ... it is recognised in short that it is among the class of the underemployed casual labourers - constituting perhaps a tenth of the whole town - that four-fifths of the problems of the Medical Officer of Health arise.[4]

The Webbs' comments were not directed simply at dock workers and nor were those of most of the other social commentators of the same period. Nevertheless, dock work was seen as an important example of casual employment and the position on the docks often was highlighted to illustrate the more general problem. For example, Henry Mayhew, writing earlier than the Webbs, reviewed casual employment in a number of industries and paid particular attention to its consequences on the docks. At one point in his review of the London poor, he described the "calling-on" system at the London docks, expressing his horror at the way men had to fight for work. He concluded:

> Until I saw with my own eyes this scene of greed and despair I could not have believed that there was so mad an eagerness to work and so biting a want of it among so vast a body of men. A day or two before I had sat at midnight in the room of a starving weaver: as I heard him tell his story there was a patience in his misery that gave it more an air of heroism than desperation. But in the scenes I have lately witnessed the want has been positively tragic and the struggle for life partaking of the sublime.[5]

One strand in the accounts of many of these social commentators was that casual employment was linked to poverty. Frequently the total income of the casual worker was too low and meant that he was living below the then accepted subsistence level. Another strand was that even when the level of income was above the subsistence level, because it was irregular, it meant that normal budgeting could not be undertaken and as a result even this higher level of income still left the worker and his family in poverty. As the Webbs and many other commentators noted, poverty was associated with poor housing, insanitary living conditions, ill-health and a variety of other social problems.

Some writers, while recognising that casual employment usually was linked to poverty, also highlighted another reason why it should cause concern. Lascelles and Bullock argued that casual employment also led to the demoralisation of the worker:

The pauperising effect of casual work is a real and serious evil, which alone would be a sufficient reason for a reform of the system. But another and perhaps more harmful product of the system is demoralisation ... It needs very little imagination to realise how the system must work for men on the fringe when unemployment is irregular and earnings low. They assemble for the first "call" at about 7.30 in the morning; the foremen appear and the preference men with the more fortunate of the casuals are duly selected. While the remainder, often the majority of the men present, remain workless for the day unless they happen to be taken on at the second call at one o'clock. It is instructive for anyone who would see the working of the system, to stand among those men when the call is over, and watch the effect of their rejection. Their disappointment is hardly ever expressed in words, and there is no outward bitterness or anger, but on all sides faces of dreary hopelessness and resigned misery. Their chance, if it ever was a chance, has come and gone, and what are they to do with the rest of the morning, or probably the rest of the day.[6]

However, Lascelles and Bullock also went on to raise another issue which directed attention away from simply the social concern felt about casual employment. They argued that casual employment also had adverse economic consequences. It left the employer with a less than satisfactory workforce: one that had lost the desire to work regularly or efficiently. They concluded: "... In the long run, such labour is far from cheap to the employers". Similar sentiments were expressed by a later government appointed committee which included employers and employees representatives amongst its members. They said:

It must be obvious that a service cannot be wholly efficient insofar as workers experience continual uncertainity in regard to their earnings with its grave social and economic consequences. Intermittent employment creates casual habits and tends to diminish the skill and output of workers.[8]

Of course, many individual employers recognised the problems created by the casual system of employment. It made it more difficult for them to build up a pool of labour that they trusted and knew could do the work efficiently. It also made it more difficult to maintain discipline. Some tried to alleviate these problems by the use of the preference system, but this was no more than a partial answer. Some also clearly believed that a more fundamental change to the system of employment would be in their own interests. Not all employers accepted this point of view: there was a strong body of opinion which saw advantage in having a surplus of labour which could be used as required and discarded when not required. However, even this view did not necessarily preclude all reforms to the system of employment. It still was possible to have a large pool of labour available for casual employment at the same time as having a defined, better organised and better disciplined pool of labour. The result was that there was considerable support amongst many employers for some changes to be made to the system of casual employment for their own sake, let alone for the benefit of dock workers, even if there was not the same enthusiasm for dock labour to be decasualised.

In fact, discussion of ways of alleviating the worst effects, both social and economic, of casual employment on the docks, took place over a prolonged period. They were first given serious consideration towards the end of the nineteenth century and came to public attention during 1889. Two events coincided in that year, the dock strike and the publication of the first two volumes of Booth's study of poverty in London. Booth himself made early proposals to deal with the problems of casual employment, though his work in the 1890's provided a more durable reform programme. This was based on a scheme introduced by the joint committee of the London and India dock companies in 1890 designed to give permanent employment to the majority of workers.

Nevertheless, these moves failed to make the hoped for progress, either initially in London, or later in Liverpool, at different times with the encouragement of Booth and Eleanor Rathbone. However, the movement for reform was given added impetus by three pieces of government legislation passed at the beginning of the twentieth century. The Port of London Act 1908 and the legislation that introduced labour exchanges in 1909[9] and health insurance in 1911[10], directly and indirectly encouraged changes in the method of employment on the docks. The Port of London Act established a new governing body for the docks, giving it, amongst other things, the duty of improving the methods of engagement of port labour. However, there was no real basis to enforce compliance and little real advance was possible in the face of resistance from employers. The labour exchange legislation enabled the Board of Trade to set up its own employment officers on the docks to deal with the particular problems of port labour. In fact, the Board of Trade sought agreement with local employers before making such moves. Discussions were held with some employers but to little effect. The health insurance legislation (unlike employment insurance), applied to dock workers from the date when it became generally operative. Under the 1911 Act the first employer in each week had to fix a stamp to the insurance card of each eligible worker: this stipulation obviously presented difficulties in an industry that was dominated by casual employment and put some pressure on employers to try to find some way of at least better organising the employment market. Section 99 of the 1911 Act enabled labour exchanges to undertake the clerical duties which might normally fall on employers in relation to health insurance if employers obtained their workers through the exchange. A number of projects were discussed on this basis though only a limited number came to fruition.

One result of these opportunities to make moves on the operation of casual labour was that attention started to be paid to the idea of registration. The idea behind registration schemes was that an attempt should be made to limit employment on the docks to those who normally sought work there on a regular basis, and to attempt to relate the number of registered workers more closely to the normal labour requirements of a particular port. Clearly registration schemes had a limited aim: they were not schemes of decasualisation. However, they were a movement to try to regularise employment and to alleviate some of the worst effects of the casual system of employment.

Liverpool Registration Scheme

The first registration scheme for dock workers in Britain was introduced in the port of Liverpool in 1912. Discussions had been started the previous year, involving employers, the union and the Board of Trade, based on the opening provided by Section 99 of the 1911 Act, and at the beginning of 1912, the Board of Trade conducted a survey of employment at the port of Liverpool. This survey showed that in January 1912, on the busiest day the maximum number of men needed was 19,900, but the number seeking work was 27,200. In addition, it was found that because of the multiplicity of "calling-on places", frequently labour demands were not met in one section of the port while there was a labour surplus in others. The survey provided the evidence needed to support the belief, already held by many leading trade unionists and employers (the initial idea for the Liverpool scheme is said to have come from James Sexton, and Liverpool shipowner, Lawrence Holt), that something had to be done to organise and regularise employment at the port.

The scheme that was adopted represented a significant modification of the proposals made in the original discussions. In its final form it was based on five principles[11]. First, a register of dock workers in the port was drawn up. The register was based on a survey of all workers who had been employed on the docks for the previous five years. Once registered the men were given a numbered tally. Second, it was agreed that the register would be controlled by a joint committee of employers and workers representatives, though most of the detailed organisational work connected with the register was undertaken by the Board of Trade. Third, surplus labour stands were erected so that workers who did not find employment at one "calling-on place" could discover more easily whether there was work elsewhere in the area. Fourth, a central clearing house was established to organise the payment of wages and insurance contributions. Fifth, the capital cost of the clearing houses, along with the wages of the staff employed in them, was to be met by the Board of Trade with employers being charged a levy amounting to about half a per cent of wages to cover the cost of running the scheme and the collection of national insurance contributions.

The scheme was not only operated in Liverpool but also was used as a model for developments in many other ports. However, it was not without its problems. For example, the number of men registered and issued with tallies was far in excess of the maximum labour demand at the port on any one day. By the end of March 1913, 31,300 tallies had been issued. Subsequently, this number was reduced (to 24,300 in 1922) and as one commentator noted, the "total number of tallies issued (did not) represent the actual number of men ready at any time to take up the job of dock work. It also (included) the sick workers as well as those who temporarily turned in their tallies in order to work for companies which (were) not members of the "docks scheme" and who (had) left the water front for other occupations"[12]. Nevertheless, the total number of tallies held by men who were actively interested in dock work remained greater than the maximum number of men required in the port at any one time for the duration of the scheme, and, as a result, the scheme could only be viewed as being partially successful in achieving its aim of regulating the availability of labour and maintaining a pool of labour close to the size of likely demand for it. A survey of dock labour at Liverpool in the mid-1930s tried to explain why the registration scheme had failed to live up to expectations on this point. It said:

> While the number of dockers available has only fallen very slowly, the trade done by the port of Liverpool representing the demand for labour, dropped very heavily after the (First World) War and has shown no signs of substantial revival. The introduction of various mechanical labour-saving devices has helped too, to reduce the amount of labour required. The result is that although the joint committee are refusing all applicants for tallies other than exceptional cases, the system of registration has made no fundamental difference to the method of casual engagement.[13]

Clearly, the reason highlighted in this survey is one explanation for the persistence of a labour surplus. However, an additional one is that the joint committee was never able to devise acceptable ways of restricting the size of the register in the first place, by refusing some men who had worked at the port a tally, and was never able to seriously attempt to review membership of the register once the scheme was under way.

The surplus stand system also encountered problems. In theory, the system should have been an important way of matching available labour with demand for it. When the scheme was first introduced provision was made for fourteen surplus stands to cover the whole of the docks. The idea was that men would first attend their normal "calling-on places" but if they were unsuccessful and unable to obtain work there, they would go to one of the surplus stands established by the Board of Trade. Employers who were unable to hire all the men they wanted at their normal "calling-on place" similarly would communicate with the nearest surplus stand (using the specially installed telephones) to see if men were available there. Although the surplus stands were used to a limited extent initially, gradually the system fell into disuse and was abandoned during the First World War: "Various reasons are given for this failure. The surplus stands cut across established custom and foremen hesitated to use the new machinery; on the other hand, workmen were under no compunction to attend or accept vacancies".[14.]

It is also important to record that the Liverpool scheme was not introduced without opposition. Many dock workers opposed the scheme and the stand taken by their own union leaders. When the scheme was introduced in July 1912, initially only a minority of dock workers registered: about 11,000 in Liverpool and a few hundred in Birkenhead. An attempt to refuse work to those who had not registered led to a strike. In Liverpool the strike was settled quickly, though a few days after the men returned to work they struck again, on that occasion not over the issue of registration itself, but because the organisational problems accompanying the introduction of the registration scheme meant that wages were paid late. The employers made concessions to persuade the men to return to work at Liverpool, but at Birkenhead, where the strike against registration itself lasted much longer, the men only returned to work when the employers recruited outside labour to do their work. Such opposition to the scheme was clearly important from a number of points of view, some of which will be explored later: at the moment it is important to record that the opposition to the scheme was one of the factors that limited the joint committee in taking action that would deal effectively with the size of the register.

Moves in Other Ports

At the same time as the registration scheme was being introduced in Liverpool similar moves were being made in other ports. For example, in Glasgow, discussions between the employers, the union (the Scottish Union of Dock Labourers) and the Board of Trade, led to a registration scheme being prepared. A local report of the discussions claimed that the: "main object of the scheme is to facilitate the working of the National Insurance Act which comes into operation in July (1912). Under the Act the employer of casual labour, which is engaged and paid off on the system which prevails at the harbour today, would find great difficulty in discharging his obligations."[15] However, it recognised that additionally the scheme would also have the benefit of improving the system of employment and increasing the status and efficiency of dock work.

The scheme itself was remarkably similar to that introduced in Liverpool. It was based on a register of dock workers and the issue of tallies, as well as clearing houses (three local and one central) and a joint committee composed of five representatives of employers, five representatives of employees and an independent chairman to run the scheme. The Board of Trade, in Glasgow as in Liverpool, was to play an important role not simply in getting discussions on the scheme started but also in administering the scheme once in operation. It was to meet the capital cost of setting up the clearing houses and was to be responsible for their operation.

In Glasgow, however, the dock workers' opposition to the scheme proved to be more formidable and decisive than it had been in Liverpool. In May of 1912, a ballot of all dock workers in Glasgow was organised, and although only a minority returned their ballot papers, of those that did, there was an overwhelming majority against the scheme (236 votes in favour, 949 votes against). The result was that the scheme was abandoned despite the fact that it had been supported by the union and the employers representatives as well as by the Board of Trade.

In fact, the movement to introduce registration schemes in other ports did not achieve a great deal until the First World War years. Schemes were introduced at Sunderland and

Goole, though they were not as sophisticated as the Liverpool scheme, and following Treasury objections, new regulations governing the adoption of schemes under Section 99 were published in December 1912 and these effectively blocked any further progress on that basis. An attempt to amend the Insurance Act, backed by Beveridge, and designed to require firms to employ only registered workers, was abandoned following resistance from within the industry. During the First World War, registration schemes were given important additional impetus. In the first few years of the war so many dock workers joined the military forces (in some cases as many as 20% of the regular labour force), that there was a danger that the ports would not be able to operate effectively and that this might hinder the war effort. One of the measures designed to deal with the problem was the establishment in early 1915 of the Port and Transit Executive. Initially this operated through controlling priorities for the discharge of goods and the use of shipping space, but later it was also able to call on special bodies of military labour to assist in dock work. Another measure was designed to ensure that dockers did not enlist in the armed forces. Dock work was added to the list of reserved occupations, but in order to determine who should be exempt from military service some attempt had to be made to determine who was and who was not a regular dock worker. The task of drawing up a list of regular dock workers was given to port labour committees, bodies composed of representatives of employers and employees. It was a short step from drawing up a list of regular dock workers to setting up some kind of scheme of registration and a step which was taken by joint committees in many ports.

In the port of Bristol, for example, a registration scheme was introduced in 1916. Although at the end of the war the scheme was reconstituted when the war agencies withdrew, the scheme continued on very similar lines to those established during the war. The scheme as reconstituted in 1919 was under the control of a joint committee, composed of five representatives of port employers, five representatives of employees and an independent chairman appointed by the Minister of Labour. The Ministry of Labour also allowed the manager of the dock employment exchange to act as secretary to the joint committee and clerical assistance was provided. The administration of the scheme, though, was in the hands of a port labour inspector who was employed and paid jointly by the employers and employees. In operation the Bristol scheme was very like the one established earlier at Liverpool: however, there were two important differences. One was that eventually the register was split in two[16]: 'A' group men were given preference for employment, while 'B' group men were only offered employment if all 'A' group men were engaged. Essentially there was an established pool of reserve labour. The second difference was that registration was dependent on union membership: a "closed shop" was enforced.

Similar schemes were established during this period at most of Britain's major ports. However, there were exceptions. One was Glasgow where a scheme of registration was prepared by the Port Labour Committee in 1917 but was eventually rejected by the Union in 1919. Another was the Tyne and Wear ports where a scheme was not introduced partly because it was believed that the geography of the ports would have made it difficult to operate a scheme effectively and partly because of opposition, particularly from dock workers. The most important port where a registration scheme was not introduced during the war, though, was London. Nevertheless, the position in London was not as hostile to registration schemes as it was in Glasgow and the Tyne and Wear ports, and, after the war, moves were made to establish a scheme in London.

The spur to action in London largely was the problem caused by the return of men after the war, many of whom were unable to enter their "old" occupations, and therefore might seek work on the docks. This threatened to make the problem of surplus labour far worse than it had been before the war. Early in 1919 a committee composed of a number of port employers and representatives was appointed with Mr Justice Roche as chairman. The committee was charged to find a solution to the problems arising from the potential influx of workers to the docks and also to examine the administration of the Out-of-Work Donation Scheme. An interim report was produced in March 1919 and following this, Ernest Bevin, who had been involved in drawing up the registration scheme in Bristol, was invited to join the committee as one of the union representatives. The final report was issued in July 1919 and recommended a voluntary registration scheme[17].

The registration scheme, following the recommendations of the Roche committee, was eventually introduced in London in February 1920. Its objectives were stated as:

(a)   To protect "bona fide" Port transport workers from unemployed workers in other trades seeking to obtain employment as Port workers.

(b)   To regulate the supply of Port labour, increase mobility where possible and provide the greatest opportunity of employment for registered workers, thereby encouraging regularity of employment for a selected body of men.

Clearly the first of these objectives, the attempt to protect dock workers from competition, was one of the reasons why dock workers in London were persuaded to accept the scheme. The basis of the London registration scheme was similar to those in operation in other ports. For example, it was run by a joint committee, registered dock workers were issued with a brass tally and a registration card, and the Ministry of Labour provided secretarial and clerical assistance. One unusual feature was that instead of an independent chairman the joint committee controlling the scheme was headed by joint chairmen (one representing the employers and one the employees).

The London registration scheme faced problems similar to those encountered in other ports. One of importance was that the number of workers registered was far in excess of the number ever likely to be employed at any one time: in London 61,000 men registered under the scheme whereas the maximum needed on any day was 34,000. Another was that the scheme was voluntary and, although in London (as in most other ports) all but a small number of employers joined the scheme, it was always possible for the terms of the scheme to be avoided. This had been made evident in the operation of the Liverpool registration scheme. For example, in 1915 the Times reported that there was a shortage of dock labour at Liverpool, and that as a result, "the restrictions (ie, registration), normally so useful in decasualising labour, have been waived, and now work at the docks is virtually thrown open to any man who seeks it."[19]

It was clear then that registration schemes were not going to solve the problems of underemployment even though they might help to alleviate them. It is also clear that dock workers' leaders would not accept registration at any price. In particular they were concerned to achieve a strong measure of union control over any registration scheme and were suspicious of state involvement. These concerns led to the failure of an initiative taken by a committee chaired by Beveridge which looked at ways in which reforms to the system of employment on the docks might be introduced under the terms of a new insurance bill which were being discussed in the summer of 1919. It is also important to recognise that for dockers' leaders the introduction of registration schemes anyway, was not their sole objective. They also wanted to introduce the idea of maintenance, that is, the idea that if dock employers needed a pool of labour available but often underemployed they should be willing to pay something to maintain this pool when no work was available.

Maintenance

Interest in maintenance amongst dock workers' unions dates back into the nineteenth century: "work or maintenance" was one of the slogans used during the 1889 dock strike. Towards the end of the First World War a maintenance scheme was put to the Government, but rejected, and a revised version of proposals made by the committee chaired by Beveridge envisaged that maintenance for dock workers could be achieved through the Unemployment Insurance Act. However, this latter proposal fared no better than the former and the Act proved to be particularly ill-suited to the need of casual workers. In an attempt to take matters forward then, the unions decided to approach the employers directly on the matter.In 1919 the National Transport Workers' Federation put forward a wage claim for dock workers which included the provision of a national minimum wage of sixteen shillings a day and maintenance based on a weekly guaranteed wage. The employers suggested that the Government should be asked to set up a court of inquiry to examine the claim (the Industrial Courts Act of 1919 had just introduced provisions for such inquiries) and after some debate the Federation agreed. The Inquiry was headed by Lord Shaw of Dunfermline and one commentator has argued that it was "one of the most significant landmarks in the history of the struggle for the improvement in the lot of dock workers"[20].

The proceedings of the Inquiry were well reported. The Federation's case was put by Ernest Bevin and was widely acclaimed. He produced a mass of evidence, including detailed case histories to show the devastating effects of the casual system of employment and then argued the case for the wage rise and maintenance.

His argument was directed to the support of two major propositions. The dockers' wages, inadequate when they were fixed in 1889, had steadily fallen behind the rising cost of living until they had become insufficient to maintain life and health, especially when the casual nature of his employment was taken into account. On the other hand, the dock employers, the shipowners and the principal industries using the docks could fully afford to pay the wages asked and to finance a system of maintenance for the men out the large profits they had made during the war, without adding a penny to the price of their goods or services.

What impressed the court and the public most was the wealth of evidence Bevin adduced to support his argument and the challenging manner in which he attacked the employers for their selfishness, their indifference to the claims of humanity and their inefficient organisation of the industry."[21]

Bevin became known as the "Dockers' KC" as the result of his presentation at the Inquiry, and the Court broadly found in favour of the Federation. In its report the Court condemned the system of casual employment.

> The court is of the opinion that labour frequently or constantly underemployed is injurious to the interests of workers, the ports, and the public, and that it is discreditable to society. It undermines all security, and is apt to undermine all self-respect on the workers' part. It is only among those who have sunk very far, and who the system itself may have demoralised, that it can be accepted as a working substitute for steady and assured employment. In one sense it is a convenience to authorities and employers, whose requirements are at the mercy of the storms and tides and unforeseen casualties, to have a reservoir of employment which can be readily tapped as the need emerges for a labour supply. If men were merely the spare parts of an industrial machine, this callous reckoning might be appropriate; but society will not tolerate much longer the continuance of the employment of human beings on these lines. The system of casualisation must, if possible, be torn up by the roots. It is wrong.[22]

The Court went on to recommend that a minimum wage of 16 shillings a day should be established for dock workers, that the principles of registration and maintenance should be accepted, that as soon as possible dock workers should be paid on a weekly basis, and that collective bargaining machinery (based on the model suggested by the Whitley Committee) should be established throughout the industry.

After the report of the Court of Inquiry the employers and the unions reached a settlement on the dock workers' claim. The employers successfully pressed the idea that wages should be based on the half-day rather than a full day, because the half-day was the traditional unit of employment on the docks. The agreement provided, therefore, for wages of eight shillings a half day (seven shillings and six pence in the smaller ports) rather than the 16 shillings a day the Court had recommended. No immediate progress was made towards the more fundamental objective of a guaranteed minimum weekly wage and maintenance. Nevertheless, these issues were now very firmly on the agenda and were to be a main focus for future discussions.

The Transport and General Workers' Union

Throughout the period under discussion important moves were taking place to try to rationalise and unify the trade unions organising dock workers. Such moves were necessary because for many years the trade unions had been split and sometimes fierce rivals. Trade unions had been established for some classes of workers on the docks before the last quarter of the nineteenth century (for example, a stevedores union had been set up in 1872) but it was not until after the 1889 dock strike that unionism spread to the mass of largely unskilled manual workers. After the strike the Dock, Wharf, Riverside and General Labourer Union was established in London with Ben Tillett, who had been secretary of a society of tea warehousemen and the original organiser of the strike, as secretary, and Tom Mann as President. The union gained widespread support in London, claiming over 30,000 members before the end of 1889, and eventually spread to some other ports, most notably Bristol. However, its membership fluctuated widely and its hold on the port of London was seriously weakened in subsequent years. Although Clegg's claim that it had been crushed twelve months after the dock strike has been challenged[23] its membership certainly declined steeply. Possibly more important, other unions were established in other ports, the most successful of which was the National Union of Dock Labourers. This union started in Glasgow but spread to other ports including Liverpool and under its secretary, James Sexton, proved to be a serious rival to the London union for many years. If the other smaller unions operating in other ports and for more specialised kinds of dock work are added to the picture then it can easily be seen the dock workers were far from united.

A number of union leaders recognised the danger of such disunity and, from the earliest days of union organisation on the docks, attempts were made to bring the unions together. For example, in 1894 an attempt was made to amalgamate the largest dock workers' unions in London and Liverpool, but this attempt failed because of opposition from the rank and file and many local union officers. In fact, it was not until 1910 that the move for unification made really serious strides forward. In that year the Dock Wharf, Riverside and General Workers' Union persuaded 36 other unions organising in the same area (this included not simply dock work but also seamen and other transport occupations) to join with them in setting up the National Transport Workers' Federation. The new body provided a basis for common action, but it left the autonomy of individual unions largely untouched, and this autonomy was jealously guarded.

The next move forward, the move that was to result in amalgamation was dependent on two main factors. The first was that in 1917 important changes were made to ease the legal requirements for union amalgamation. Under the Trade Union (Amalgamation) Act of that year it was determined that in future amalgamations could proceed, provided that 50 per cent of all union members entitled to vote did so in a ballot on the amalgamation proposals and providing that a 20 per cent majority of those voting was gained for the amalgamation proposals. The second was that a mechanism was devised, based largely on the experience of American unions[24], for amalgamation to proceed but for individual trades to retain some autonomy. This was what became the trade group system of the Transport and General Workers' Union.

In addition to these two main factors, attention also needs to be given to a third, the impact of the Shaw Inquiry. The results of this inquiry gave added weight to the argument for common action, at least on the part of the dockers' unions, and also brought Ernest Bevin to prominence. The emergence of Bevin as a national figure enabled him to take a leading part in the amalgamation movement. While this third factor was obviously only of importance in the later stages of the amalgamation movement, it was possibly of crucial importance at that time.

The moves that led to amalgamation started in 1920. In July of that year a resolution supporting amalgamation of transport workers' unions was passed at a meeting of the National Transport Workers' Federation. As a result of this resolution, a committee was set up consisting of representatives from the Dock, Wharf, Riverside and General Workers' Union and the National Union of Dock, Riverside and General Workers, with Harry Gosling (not a member of either union, but president of the Transport Workers' Federation) as chairman. Eventually, other unions were drawn into the discussions and in December of 1920, an amalgamation scheme was proposed. Ballots were held in 20 unions, and, in 14 of them, the legal requirements for amalgamation were met. In May of 1921 eleven of these unions decided to support amalgamation and the Transport and General Workers' Union came into operation on 1 January 1922. A provisional executive was elected with Harry Gosling as President and Ernest Bevin as General Secretary.

It would be difficult to overestimate the importance of the amalgamation for the future conduct of affairs on the docks. Not only did the amalgamation ease the rivalry between workers' organisations, but it also set the pattern for the future in other ways. First, it did so by ensuring that in the future most dock workers would not be members of a union that solely represented them or their interests: they were to be members of a union that represented a range of transport workers and eventually workers from a wide variety of different occupations. This meant that to a certain extent their interests were not all that was to determine policy making: at times they had to be willing to subordinate their own interests to those of other sections. Sometimes as well it meant that the leaders of the union were not simply concerned, when framing policy or taking action, with the reaction of dock workers but also were concerned with the reaction of the whole body of the membership, even when the issue was solely of immediate concern to the dock workers. Second, although there were important restrictions on the actions of dock workers and their leaders, because of the adoption of the trade groups' method of organisation, dockers nevertheless still had considerable autonomy. It was an autonomy which was guarded not simply by dockers but also by other groups in the unions. Third, the election of Ernest Bevin as General Secretary in the new union ensured that dock workers would have somebody vitally interested in their affairs and with strong views on how they should be dealt with at the head of the union. Bevin had been concerned with the organisation of dockers for much of his union career, both at Bristol and London, and when the Transport and General Workers' Union was formed, he became national secretary of the trade group covering dock workers.

Reactions to Attempts at Reform

The setting up of the Transport and General Workers' Union was an important event in its own right and an important influence on the direction of moves to reform the casual system of employment on the docks. Another important influence was the reactions of various people and parties to reform attempts. Some of these reactions have been noted already, but they are of sufficient importance to warrant separate and more detailed treatment.

Earlier, it was noted that many dock employers saw some advantage in schemes of registration. Not all dock employers did so, and a number tried to avoid the provisions of registration schemes once they were established. Nevertheless, the support of many dock employers for registration was important: in some instances they took the lead in putting forward registration schemes. In Glasgow, for example, the employers continually pressed for registration and although this pressure found some support amongst union leaders it found little amongst dock workers.

Government agencies also played a role in the establishment of registration schemes. Initially the Board of Trade played a major role in securing the introduction of registration schemes in a number of ports. Some of their officials seemed personally committed to the idea of registration and initiated discussions on the matter between employers and unions. Later the Board of Trade and the Ministry of Labour gave practical help to registration schemes, in particular over their administration. The Government also encouraged registration schemes during the First World War more specifically by its attempts to control manpower and ensure the efficient operation of the ports so as not to hinder the war effort. However, the Government seemed unwilling to take a firm lead in the absence of support from the industry itself. Many initiatives and openings provided by the Government came to nothing because of the absence of support from within the industry.

The influence and support of social reformers was also important. Their descriptions of the social conditions of dock workers encouraged others to take action. The Liverpool scheme of 1912, for example, was in part devised as a reaction to the reports prepared by people like Eleanor Rathbone[25].

However, because of the focus of later discussion, the reactions of dockers and the unions to these early schemes of registration and maintenance are particularly important. The reaction of leaders and members frequently differed and were a constant potential source of conflict.

Some union leaders displayed an open hostility to attempts that were made to deal with casual employment. Probably the best example is provided by Ben Tillett, one of the London dockers' leaders. He saw the schemes put forward as being designed solely to benefit employers. In the Annual Report of the Dock, Wharf, Riverside and General Workers' Union for 1912, he wrote:

> The government is at present busy on some scheme to dragoon so-called unskilled dockers into "clearing house schemes", which make the employers a greater tyrant than ever, and leave men for everlasting at the beck and call of foremen and managers who are too incapable or too indolent to organise the labour in their charge to advantage.[26]

However, such views were not typical, certainly of the major national leaders. A number of prominent union leaders not only supported and negotiated for schemes of registration and maintenance, but also were deeply committed to them as a way of helping to decasualise dock work. James Sexton, for example, the Liverpool dockers' leader, fought for schemes of registration to be adopted in his own port. He clearly believed that they were of crucial importance in improving the conditions of dock workers. In his autobiography, he wrote that such schemes were a "tremendous boon" and would be supported by "any sane person"[27].

Possibly more important was the case of Ernest Bevin. He had been convinced of the need to take action to deal with casual employment on the docks from his early days in the union in Bristol. He had played a major role in drawing up the registration scheme at Bristol and later played a similarly important role in drawing up the London scheme. There was no doubt that he saw such schemes as valuable, but as one of his biographers, Bullock, notes, he saw them as only a first step:

> Bevin never viewed registration as anything more than a first step which would be ineffectual unless it were accompanied by two other measures: a reduction of the numbers registered to a figure more approaching the actual needs of the port and much more efficient arrangements for the transfer of labour from one dock to another within the port. Even then there was bound to be unemployment during slack periods, and Bevin argued that this could only be dealt with by the decasualisation of the industry and the provision of a guaranteed minimum wage.[28]

Bevin, then, was keen to ensure that once registration schemes had been established they would be made effective and followed by maintenance. Bullock went on to argue that Bevin pursued decasualisation persistently over a period of twenty years, and although it would be wrong to argue that it was his only or consuming interest (for as leader of a major union he dealt with a variety of trades and issues) he retained a personal interest in the dock workers' cause throughout his life and retained a commitment to press for measures that would help to decasualise the port transport industry. Bevin's commitment was in part the result of the belief that casual work led to unacceptable social conditions and in part the result of his early association with dock workers, an association which was cemented through his presentation of their case at the Shaw Inquiry, an event which meant that he became identified as "the" dock workers' leader.

It needs to be stressed, however, that particularly in the early years, even in the case of dockers' leaders who supported moves to deal with casual employment, that commitment to decasualisation schemes in general and registration in particular was conditional. Some of the earliest schemes for extending permanent employment were met with opposition by union leaders. For example, Sexton opposed proposals that would have resulted in the classification of dock workers, as did union leaders in London. Phillips and Whiteside argue that for union leaders, "decasualisation in itself was neither desirable or undesirable; it was good or bad according to its likely reaction upon the strength and security of their own organisations"[29]. Thus, union leaders supported the 1912 Liverpool scheme, whereas they had opposed some earlier initiatives in the same port primarily in order to buttress its own organisation and exclude non-unionists from the docks, not to promote decasualisation per se. It supported the 1912 scheme, "because it confirmed the negotiating rights it had won in the strike of the year before and conceded joint control over registration. Its enthusiasm was redoubled when the distribution of tallies was placed in its charge"[30]. During the war a similar explanation can be put forward for union support for schemes in other ports:

> In the Bristol Channel, in particular, Ernest Bevin successfully cast the branches of his union in the role of registrars, and rendered membership a necessary condition of employment. In Swansea, for example, the Dockers' Union made its card, and later its badge, the emblem of registration (while the efforts of the Board of Trade to introduce a more orthodox system of tallies were blocked). Military exemption was also confined to trade unionists, both in South Wales and on Merseyside.[31]

The importance that union leaders gave to either their control or their joint control of the registration system cannot be overstated. Nor should it be overlooked that registration could be a valuable weapon in strengthening union membership moving towards the closed shop.

In some cases this was a question of persuading nonmembers to join, in others it was a question of one union trying to gain advantage at the expense of another. For example, it has been argued that this was particularly the case in two of the Welsh ports, Cardiff and Newport[32]. It would be wrong, though, to let these considerations drive out recognition that many union leaders genuinely believed that decasualisation was a desirable social reform, one that would be in the long term interests of their members, and one that was worth fighting for.

The commitment of union leaders like Bevin to moves such as registration and maintenance, which might reform the casual system of employment stands in stark contrast to the ambivalence and sometimes outright hostility of many dock workers to them. Such hostility was shown from the very beginning. For example, note has already been taken of the opposition to the registration scheme introduced in Liverpool in 1912, in part evidenced by the strikes against the schemes. The leading union figure in Liverpool at the time, James Sexton, instituted libel proceedings against the authors of a pamphlet who said that through registration he had conspired to hand over the union to the employers. In his autobiography, Sexton described in detail the problems he encountered dealing with his own union members over this issue. In one passage he recalls how the union decided to hold meetings to try to explain to the dockers what the scheme would mean to them, but often when he tried to speak he was refused a hearing:

> On one occasion, indeed, I had to get police protection and on another I had to escape by way of the roof.[33]

Sexton also recalled how the union held a ballot to test reaction to the scheme, and although they obtained a majority in support, those who opposed the scheme had persuaded most dockers not to vote, so that in the end only 12 per cent of those eligible to vote did so. Sexton's description of the opposition shown by many dockers to registration was confirmed by other commentators. The Times, reviewing events surrounding the Liverpool strike also noted that such opposition often turned to violence, though in one report it seemed a little disappointed that events were not more spectacular. It said:

> The only exciting incident of the day was a raid on the offices of the National Union of Dock Labourers by two men, one of whom threatened violence to general secretary, Mr James Sexton, but made off without putting the threat into execution.[34]

Taplin lays some of the blame for the opposition of the Liverpool dockers on the shoulders of Sexton himself. He argues that he failed to consult his members properly: thus, "Sexton chose to ignore one of the most sensitive features of the Liverpool dock labourer: his right to be consulted"[35]. He also suggests that those on the Liverpool docks who were opposed to Sexton and his style of leadership found in the registration proposal a useful hook on which to hang their attacks. One of these opponents in particular used the links between Sexton and the shipowners in putting forward the scheme as a way of attacking both the scheme and Sexton. Thus it was argued: "the very fact that the scheme is put forward by such eminent - dockers please note - men of business as Mr Harold Sanderson, Mr A A Booth, Mr H W Nelson and Mr James Sexton, should be quite sufficient to convince every docker that this scheme will certainly be a boon to the shipowners of Liverpool"[36].

Taplin points out that although Sexton congratulated himself that opposition to registration disappeared once the strike was over and the scheme had started, there is evidence that at least some opposition persisted for a number of years. This view is given credence by a letter published in the Liverpool Daily Post and Mercury in July 1914, in which a docker complained that the registration scheme "possessed only one object - viz, to keep the docker in a ring: in other words to tie him up to the shipowner"[37].

However, opposition to registration by dockers was not confined to Liverpool and is not simply explicable by its association with Sexton. The Dockers' Record reported that in Hull: "the scheme of registration is cordially detested by the men"[38].

In some ports the opposition was overcome and the schemes were eventually introduced, but, as has been noted, in others the opposition was so strong that attempts to introduce registration schemes were abandoned. This happened most spectacularly at Glasgow, first in 1912 and again in 1919.

The opposition of many dock workers to registration schemes led some supporters of such schemes to express exasperation. Thus, one commentator wrote about the strikes in Liverpool against the 1912 scheme:

> Whenever the improvement of the condition of the working classes is under consideration it is always assumed that the influence to be counteracted is a relentless, bloodless, competitive system, conducted in the interest of capital, under which wealth accumulates and men decay. The eager social reformer is apt to leave altogether out of account the folly and perversity of those whose lot he is so zealous to improve, and yet this perversity and folly constitute a very ponderable factor in the problem as may be seen from the strike which has just been declared by the dock workers of Liverpool against the recently inaugurated house scheme.
>
> No more entirely beneficent measure than the clearing house has ever been devised. No measure has commanded more disinterested and devoted thought on the part of employers for their employed ...
>
> This admirable scheme, which to their credit, the shipowners at once accepted, might have been expected to inspire the enthusiasm of the men for whose advantage it was signally contrived. It had, indeed, the hearty support of the Dockers' Union and, indeed, its elaboration owed not a little to the cooperation of Mr James Sexton, the enlightened General Secretary of the Union. But in spite of all persuasions, the men, darkly suspicious from the first, have now revolted - thus blindly with their blessedness at strife.[39]

Other commentators tried to explain the attitude of dock workers who opposed registration. It was noted, for example, that some dockers liked the freedom to work when and where they wanted and believed that registration schemes would inhibit such freedom. The report of the Shaw Inquiry argued that many dockers "have got into the habit of thinking that day labour is a sign of independence, and that day labour secured even for a week leaves them devoid of that liberty to do nothing they have come to prize"[40]. Another commentator suggested that dockers were a race apart who took a pride in their strength and skill and bred the same attitudes into their sons: "They looked upon their freedom to work hard for two or three days, then to 'play', as a superior state to the monotony and discipline of work in a factory"[41] It was also argued that some dockers saw registration schemes as instruments of discipline and coercion, solely of value to the employers. More generally it was noted that dock workers disliked any kind of control: some likened registration to being branded like cattle. The dockers at Glasgow who opposed registration also fought the introduction of national insurance cards because they feared the control it implied. Whatever the reasons, and whether the fears were real or imaginary, the opposition or at least the scepticism of many dock workers, towards registration schemes during this period is widely acknowledged and stands in contrast to the views and policies of the official union leaders.

None of this means that dockers were unable to recognise the problems created by casual employment and were not at times keen to voice them. Insecurity of income caused many problems even if some could be overcome by domestic and community arrangements. Dockers were not a homogeneous group and some could deal with these problems better than others. The point, though, is that financial security was not valued above all else and for many dockers was not a sufficient attraction to overcome their opposition to decasualisation.

A Pattern for the Future

The moves made to alleviate the worst effects of the use of the casual system of employment in the port transport industry prior to the setting up of the Transport and General Workers' Union were important, if for no other reason, because they helped to establish the pattern for the future. This can be seen in a number of different areas.

First, the moves made to establish schemes of registration and maintenance schemes during the 1912 to 1922 period were to be continued until after the Second World War. Although the details varied, the idea that conditions on the docks should be improved by seeking the adoption of such schemes was broadly accepted. This was seen to be the best way forward, even if it was not seen as a solution to all of the problems, which some believed could only be fully dealt with by decasualisation.

Second, these moves to establish registration and maintenance schemes were most strongly supported by the dockers' union leaders. Many employers also supported registration schemes (though most thought they should be voluntary rather than compulsory) but they were less enthusiastic about maintenance, especially if the cost was to fall on them. Nevertheless, the trade unions pressed for both of these measures and the enthusiasm of senior officials of the main union, the Transport and General Workers' Union, rarely waned.

Third, many dockers remained suspicious of moves to introduce registration and maintenance schemes, though suspicion of the latter was largely motivated by the belief (generally supported) that you could not have maintenance without registration. The suspicion on the part of many dockers of any moves to decasualise dock work, which was first felt during the earliest attempts to introduce registration schemes, was to continue for many decades.

Notes

1. See, for example, J Tunstall, *The Fishermen,* MacGibbon & Kee, London, 1962.
2. Often referred to as "the turn". There were some exceptions to this employment pattern but they were relatively insignificant.
3. See, for example, E C P Lascelles, S S Bullock, *Dock Labour and Decasualisation,* P S King, London, 1924.
4. S & B Webb, *The Minority Report of the Poor Law Commission,* Longman, Green & Co, London, 1909, p191.
5. H Mayhew, *London Labour and the London Poor,* Griffin, Brown & Co, London, 1861, p313.
6. *Op Cit,* p60.
7. *Ibid,* p62.
8. MacLean Committee report, presented to the Minister of Labour, 1931, p10.
9. Employment Exchanges Act, 1909.
10. National Insurance Act, 1911.
11. Description based on E C P Lascelles and S S Bullock, Op Cit and J Sexton, Agitator, Faber & Faber, London, 1936.
12. Monthly Labour Review.
13. See J Sexton, *Op Cit.*

14. *Ibid,* p36.
15. Glasgow Herald, 27 April 1912, p12.
16. This was not part of the initial scheme but a later development.
17. Neither report was published.
18. Port of London Registration Committee, Review of the London Registration Scheme, 1925, p3.
19. Times, 6 June 1915, p5.
20. V H Jensen, *The Hiring of Dock Workers,* Harvard University Press, Cambridge (Mass), 1964, p125.
21. A Bullock, *The Life and Times of Ernest Bevin,* Vol 1, Heinemann, London, 1964, pp 122-123.
22. Court of Inquiry into Transport Workers, HMSO, London, 1920, Cd 93617.
23. Transport and General Workers Union, *Record,* September 1964, pp 36-39.
24. Bevin visited the USA and studied the structure of unions there and was said to have been strongly influenced by what he saw. Other trade union leaders prominent in setting up the Transport and General Workers Union also visited the USA and were said to have been similarly impressed.
25. E Rathbone, *Inquiry into the Conditions of Labour at the Liverpool Docks,* Liverpool Economic and Statistical Society, 1903-4.
26. G Phillips, N Whiteside, *Casual Labour,* Clarendon Press, Oxford, 1985, pp 100-101.
27. *Op Cit,* p226.
28. *Op Cit,* p120.
29. *Op Cit,* p63.
30. *Ibid,* p95.
31. *Ibid,* p127.
32. *Ibid,* p150.
33. *Op Cit,* p227.
34. Times, 16 July 1912, p6.
35. E Taplin, *The Dockers' Union,* Leicester UP, 1986, p112.
36. *Ibid,* p114.
37. *Ibid,* p115.
38. July, 1917.
39. Letter to Times, 18 July 1912, p8, by R Heald, former editor of Liverpool Courier.
40. *Ibid,* p17.
41. A Bullock, *Op Cit,* p117.

3 The interwar years

The amalgamations which led to the creation of the Transport and General Workers Union brought new strength to trade unionism on the docks. The earlier attempts at cooperation had never been entirely satisfactory and the new union seemed to offer a better opportunity to press for improvement in the conditions of employment of the dock worker. The pattern for attempts to reform the casual system had already been set: registration and mainten nce were firmly on the agenda. The interwar years did bring major strikes forward, but initially the new union was faced with attacks on the gains that had been made at the Shaw Inquiry.

Wage Reduction

The amalgamation of unions to form the Transport and General Workers' Union followed the successful outcome of the Shaw Inquiry[1]. The wage increases gained as a result of that inquiry, however, were short lived. The rate of 16 shillings a day recommended by the Shaw Inquiry was reduced to 12 shillings a day and, early in 1922, almost immediately following the formal establishment of the Transport and General Workers' Union, the employers demanded a further wage reduction of two shillings a day, or changes in working conditions and the length of the working week. Bevin, who at that time was National Secretary of the docks group as well as General Secretary of the union, persuaded the union to oppose any changes in working practices or the length of the working week, arguing that these would be much more difficult to recoup at a later date than a wage reduction. In fact, the wage reduction was staggered; wages were reduced by one shilling a day in October 1922 and a further shilling a day in June 1923.

The wage reduction itself was of no direct significance for the movement to deal with the problems relating to the casual system of employment. However, the reaction of some dockers to the wage reduction was of more importance for it gave an indication of the more general problems the Transport and General Workers' Union was going to face in relation with its own members. In fact, the first stage of the wage reduction passed with little trouble, but the second stage brought serious conflict in a number of ports. At the beginning of July 1923 dock workers in Hull went on strike against the wage reduction, and their action was soon mirrored in London, Grimsby, Liverpool and South Wales.

The strikes against the wage reduction were over relatively quickly in most ports, though in London they lasted for seven weeks. However, the length of the strikes is not the most important factor. More important is that the strikers reserved most of the wrath not for the employers but for their own leaders. Bevin, in particular, was the subject of personal abuse and forced to watch as a meeting of London dockers passed a resolution expressing no confidence in him. Even more significant, though, was that a number of London dockers left the Transport and General Workers' Union to join one of the small unions which had not amalgamated with the other dockers unions in 1922, the Amalgamated Stevedores' Protection League. The union was then renamed the National Amalgamated Stevedores, Lightmen, Watermen and Dockers Union and was to become a constant source of friction for the Transport and General Workers' Union.

Moves to reverse the wage reduction started within months of the London strike being settled. The state of the economy was more favourable by the end of 1923; in November a National Dock Delegate conference agree to claim an extra 2 shillings a day and when the employers replied with an offer of 1 shilling a day in January 1924 the dockers turned it down. The following month the dockers went on strike, but the strike lasted for only 10 days. The employers gave way on the wage claim; however, more significantly for the moves to deal with the casual system of employment the agreement that ended the strike also provided for the setting up of a joint committee to inquire into the problem of decasualisation and maintenance.

In a report to the national executive committee of the Transport and General Workers' Union Bevin laid stress on the importance of the action taken on decasualisation. However, he argued that agreement with the employers was not enough by itself.

> This social sore (decasualisation) must be removed. In this connection, however, it has to be borne in mind that not only is it necessary to reach agreements with the Port Labour Employers, but that legislation is also required. Accordingly, a Bill has been drafted ..... and deposited in the House of Commons. Bro. Ben Smith, having been fortunate in the ballot for Private Members' Bills will move it at the first available opportunity.[2]

Bevin also organised meetings with Government ministers to press their case for legislation and lobbied Members of Parliament to support Smith's bill. In fact, the bill failed to make the hoped for progress, partly because of the prolonged Parliamentary discussion on proportional representation. For the time being, then, Bevin and the Transport and General Workers' Union had to abandon their attempts to achieve changes to the system of employment on the docks through legislation, though Bevin never abandoned the quest for legislation in the long term. The immediate future, though, was given over to joint moves with the employers.

Maclean Committee

Clause 9 of the February 1924 Agreement between the Transport and General Workers' Union and the National Council of Port Labour Employers said:

47

9. Decasualisation - The parties to this Agreement agree to appoint a sub-committee (the Minister of Labour to appoint an independent chairman and supply such technical assistance as may be necessary) for the purpose of developing and strengthening the system of registration and to examine the proposal for a guaranteed week with a view to aiming at an agreement to give effect to the Shaw Report.[3]

The committee was duly set up and Sir Donald Maclean was appointed as Chairman. The Transport and General Workers' Union was represented by Ernest Bevin, James Sexton and Ben Tillett.

The Committee issued two interim reports, one in June and the other in July 1924. The first interim report reviewed the progress so far towards introducing registration schemes in all ports. It was noted that such schemes were operating in 17 ports including Liverpool, London, Manchester and Southampton, and one was in the process of being introduced in another port.[4] However, schemes had not been introduced in 33 other ports, including the Humber ports, the Tyne and Wear ports and Glasgow. It was recommended that in those ports that did not have a registration scheme in operation "steps should at once be taken jointly by employers and workers in these ports with a view to (the introduction of a scheme) at the earliest date possible."[5] It was further recommended that in those ports where registration schemes were already being operated, and once such schemes were introduced in other ports, attempts should be made to periodically review the register so as to remove men who did not regularly seek work on the docks and so as to reduce the register to a size which meant that the number of dockers on the register was close to the number demanded by port employers.

The issue of maintenance and the guaranteed working week was raised in the second interim report. However, in that report it was argued that:

In regard to the proposal for a guaranteed week, in whatever form it may be examined, the basic question is one of cost. This question cannot be determined, however, without knowing the number of men who normally and regularly seek, their livelihood at the docks .... Such information cannot be forthcoming until an effective system of registration is established and the registers are so revise as to include only men who have a valid claim to be registered.[6]

The committee offered to assist any port that experienced difficulties introducing a registration scheme and urged the National Joint Council for Dock Labour to press the recommendations made in the first interim report. Nevertheless, it is clear that the Maclean Committee made little real headway on the question on maintenance as such.

The failure to make progress on the guaranteed week angered some sections of the union. One area committee [7] passed a resolution early in 1925 saying that the agreement that brought the 1924 strike to an end had not been put into effect properly and urging the Executive Council to take all necessary steps to enforce the Guaranteed Week at an early date. However, Bevin, and the General Executive Council believed that little more could be done at that time, partly because of economic conditions. As a result in February 1925 the General Executive Council passed a resolution which said:

This Council is satisfied that the pledges referred to (which were contained in the agreement that led to the return to work following the strike in early 1924) have not been broken, and that no undue delay is taking place in the establishment of the principle of maintenance having regard to the difficulties to be overcome and the fact that it is necessary in the first place to thoroughly settle the question of Registration.[8]

For about the next five years attention was concentrated on the question of registration rather than maintenance; the latter item was not forgotten, nor abandoned by the Transport and General Workers' Union as a long term aim, but it was accepted that it could not claim priority until the question of registration had been settled. In fact, registration schemes were established at many ports during this period. They had been set up at Ardrossan, Barry, Cardiff, Dundee, Fowey, Middlesborough, Port Talbot and Workington by the end of 1924; in the following two years they were established at Ayr, Barrow, Garston, Goole, Grangemouth, Greenock, Grimsby, Hull, Leith and Newport (Mon), and a scheme was introduced in Swansea in 1927. In other ports, where schemes were in existence before the Maclean Committee was set up revisions were made to try to make them more effective; for example, in London the registration committee was reconstituted in 1925 and undertook a complete review of the register in line with the recommendation of the first interim report of the Maclean Committee.

The details of the schemes operating in the different ports varied. For example, in some ports registration meant the use of a special registration book or card, in others it meant the use of a tally. Similarly, there were differences in terms of which workers were covered by the registration scheme (in some ports clerical workers, time-keepers and checkers, boiler-scalers, riggers, coal porters, warehousemen, cranedrivers and foreman stevedores were covered whereas in other ports they were not). Again in some ports union membership was compulsory for registration, whereas in other ports it was not.

It is also important to note that the story was n t simply one of progress towards registration schemes being established in all ports. Over the same period as many ports were setting up registration schemes others were abandoning them. Thus, Aberdeen, Hartlepool, Lowestoft and Great Yarmouth, all had schemes in operation at the time when the Maclean Committee was set up but abandoned them over the next few years. Further, a number of ports which did not have registration schemes at the time when the Maclean Committee was set up failed to establish such schemes in the subsequent four years; these ports included Glasgow and the Tyne and Wear ports.

It is also worthwhile recording that by the end of the 1920s, despite the fact that considerable progress had been made in the move to establish registration schemes, such schemes were operating far from perfectly. There were a number of difficulties. One was that in many ports little progress had been made in bringing the number of men on the register more closely into line with the demand for labour. London was an exception; the review of the register undertaken in 1925 and referred to above, meant that by 1930 the number of men had been reduced to 36,000, as opposed to the 62,000 on the register in 1920. However, in most other ports such reviews did not take place with the result that there was constantly a considerable surplus of men on the register over what was required in the port. For example, large surpluses existed in both Liverpool and Hull and one report argued that i Hull, the registration scheme had "done nothing to reduce the surplus"[9] of dockers.

One of the reasons (but by no means the only one) why registers were so large was that the available labour was not used efficiently because there was little mobility of labour. In many ports workers tended to work simply in one area or on one particular kind of work, a practice which was encouraged by many employers. Generally, men did not move from one part of the port or from one type of work to another when work was short in one section but plentiful in another. As a result, a review on the operation of registration schemes at the end of the 1920s noted:

.... Local surpluses of registered men are common, and these surpluses may exist side by side with the employment of non-registered labour at other spots where the number of registered men is temporarily short.[10]

Bevin clearly saw this as a major problem. In his annual report for 1927 he was able to review the success achieved in pressing for the establishment of registration schemes, but had to temper this with a warning that the retention of a large number of call places and the consequent hindrance to mobility was preventing them "carrying forward the work of decasualisation in as rapid a manner as it would be possible to do under different circumstances."[11]

Maintenance and Re-convened Maclean Committee

The moves to establish registration schemes after the interim reports of the Maclean Committee, then, met with mixed success. Such schemes were established in most large ports and by 1930 covered almost 90,000 dock workers (approaching 70 per cent of the total). However, the schemes were not operating as effectively as many would have liked and one or two major ports had failed to adopt a scheme.

Registration, though, was only one of the aims of the dock worker. Another and in some ways more fundamental one was maintenance. The second aim was never lost sight of by the Transport and General Workers' Union; they supported registration schemes in part because they were seen as a necessary forerunner to maintenance. In fact, while the union was in the middle of pressing ports to adopt effective registration schemes, Bevin was already calling on the employers to consider how maintenance might be introduced. In 1926 he issued a memorandum on maintenance in which he called for experiments in a number of ports to see how maintenance might operate. The ports he suggested were London, Bristol, Manchester, Liverpool and Southampton. In London and Manchester, he wanted a proportion of men to be offered permanent employment with other men being offered a guarantee of four days work (or equivalent earnings) a week. In Bristol, Liverpool and Southampton, he wanted all men to be offered a guarantee of four days work, or equivalent earnings each week. Bevin recognised that the cost of the scheme was a crucial issue. He suggested that the costs might be met in two ways.

(1)   The port undertaking such a scheme must bear some cost which would be compensated for in increased efficiency and regularity of labour. It would indeed actually save in cost of social services, if labour was definitely regulated. The cost should be a diminishing one in-so-far as the ports are concerned, as there are men at present working up to 60 and 70 hours a week whilst others obtain only one or two days ...

(2)   Then comes the question of the contribution from the Government. The Government should be willing to contribute an annual sum over a period of years equal to what they have contributed to the Unemployment Fund during say each of the past two years, and have the right to examine what becomes of the make-up amount. At the end of a period of say 3 years, the sum contributed by the Government could be reviewed in the light of changes and developments which would have taken place in the meantime.[12]

The Transport and General Workers' Union also submitted evidence and a case for special treatment of dock workers to the Blanesburgh Committee [13] which had been established to review the working of the unemployment insurance scheme but the committee's report like the employers' reaction to Bevin's memorandum, was a disappointment to the union: according to Bevin, "whilst a few pious words were inserted in the report, no real recommendation was made on the evidence we submitted".[14]

Nevertheless, the Transport and General Workers' Union continued to press the case for maintenance, and the concern felt generally, and expressed with some emphasis by the port employers, about the way the unemployment insurance was working in the case of dock workers, gave them a lever to keep pressing the issue.

Dock workers had been brought within the provisions of unemployment insurance in 1920 when the scheme was extended to cover all manual workers earning not more than £250 a year, and in 1921 conditions were relaxed to make them more attractive to dockers. The provisions of the unemployment insurance scheme meant that workers who suffered continuous unemployment for three days or more were able to claim benefit, and for the purpose of calculation any three days of unemployment whether consecutive or not, within a period of six consecutive days, was treated as a continuous period of unemployment. In most industries this provision caused few problems because employment was usually by the week, and therefore except when 'short time' was being operated a worker would not expect to switch between employment and unemployment on different days of the week. In the port transport industry, though, this was not the case: because employment frequently was still by the half day most dockers expected to alternate between employment and unemployment swiftly and from day to day. As the Ministry of Labour had argued this had important implications for the operation of unemployment insurance.

> In the Port Transport Industry employment for shorter periods than a week is the common experience of large classes of workers. This under-employment has an effect both on Unemployment Insurance contributions and benefits. So far as contributions are concerned it has the effect that, as contributions are paid weekly n respect of any period of employment from half a day upwards, the amount of contributions paid is sometimes high in proportion to the work done. On the other hand, industries carried on on a casual basis have a much higher rate of umemployment than those providing regular employment, with the result that the latter industries pay a higher rate of contribution than is required by their low rate of unemployment, and the former pay a lower rate than is required by their high rate of unemployment.[15]

In part, then, the argument was that because of the nature of employment practices on the docks one would expect that most dock workers would be able to claim unemployment insurance benefits certainly more frequently than was the case with workers in other industries. However, the employers extended this argument by suggesting that in certain instances the provisions of unemployment insurance encouraged dockers not to work even when employment was available: in particular they argued that the way the regulations about continuous unemployment were interpreted acted as an inducement for dockers to avoid employment in cases where if they accepted employment their continuity would be broken. This position was aggravated in 1930 when the provisions of an Act passed in that year meant that if the Ministry of Labour wished to disqualify a worker from benefit because he was not willing to accept employment when it was available, the onus of proof lay not with the worker but with the officer of the Ministry of Labour.

The concern about the operation of the unemployment insurance eventually led to the Government in 1930 to ask the Maclean Committee (it had met on a number of occasions after producing its two interim reports in 1924) to reconvene. It was asked:

> To enquire into employment and unemployment in the port transport services in Great Britain, and to make recommendations thereon, with special reference to decasualisation and the administration of the Unemployment Insurance Scheme and in its application to port transport workers.[16]

In practice the committee dealt with two issues, the operation of registration schemes and the problems arising from the arrangements for unemployment insurance. On both of these issues there was broad agreement over certain matters; however, when it came to making recommendations the committee was split with the employers and the trade union representatives putting forward different solutions to the problems in both major areas.

For example, when the committee considered the issue of registration all members were able to agree on the desirability of registration schemes. Thus, the committee was able to report:

> Having been able by the above means (collecting evidence on the operation of all schemes) to make an exhaustive study of the principles and operation of registration, we have no hesitation in recording our view that it is a satisfactory and essential first step in the decasualisation of port labour. In actual operation it is apparent that it has succeeded in bringing some measure of order out of chaos and that it is a necessary foundation for any ther steps which may be taken still further to regularise port employment.[17]

The committee were also able to agree that an extension of registration schemes to all ports was desirable. They argued that:

> In our opinion no port can hope to make any real progress towards regularisation of port employment without a registration scheme ... We have no hesitation, therefore, in re-affirming that a jointly administered registration scheme is the only satisfactory foundation upon which to build hopes of eventual decasualisation.[18]

However, when the committee came to consider how registration schemes should be extended and administered then fundamental differences of approach came to the surface. The employers representatives argued that the previous basis of operation should be continued; that is, attempts should be made to persuade employers and unions in all ports to introduce registration schemes and to operate them jointly but there should be no attempt to compel them to introduce a scheme and the scheme itself should be voluntary. The Transport and General Workers' Union took a different view. They favoured an all-embracing national statutory scheme which would replace the numerous local and voluntary ones.

At the end of the day there was no real attempt to bring these different views together. The nearest thing to an attempt to reconcile the different views was the memorandum of the chairman. He suggested that time should be given to see if voluntary schemes would be introduced effectively in all ports. However, if after 5 years registration schemes were not operating in all major ports then statutory powers should be sought to attain that end.

A similar pattern of general agreement over problems but disagreement over solutions held when the committee moved from the consideration of registration to look at the issue of unemployment insurance. The Ministry of Labour presented the committee with a range of statistics showing the way the unemployment insurance scheme was operation in the port transport industry. For example, they showed that on 27th October 1930, out of approximately 168,000 insured people employed in the 'Dock, Harbour, River and Canal Service', 63,400 (or about 34%) were unemployed. Of course, many of the workers recorded as being unemployed were not necessarily unemployed for the whole of the week; the record simply referred to one particular day and many dockers experienced unemployment at some time during a week but were employed for the rest of it. Nevertheless, this figure gave some indication of the extent of underemployment in the industry. Other statistics presented to the committee related more centrally to unemployment insurance and attempted a more direct measure of the extent to which unemployment insurance was claimed by dockers. Thus, it was shown that between 1921 and 1929 (inclusive) about £6 million had been contributed to the unemployment insurance fund (by employers, employees and the state together) on behalf of the dockers, while nearly £22 million was paid out in benefit to them. The explanation offered for the relatively large amount paid out in benefit was that the operation of the "continuity rule" meant that many ockers who were underemployed rather than unemployed for long periods were able to claim benefit. An analysis of the position in one port, London, for the insurance year 1929-30 illustrated what was happening. In that year 34,315 insured port workers came within the scope of the London Registration Scheme. Of these, 28,761 had 40 or more insurance contributions though in a large proportion of cases the contributions had been paid in respect of less than a full week's employment and a number of men were only employed for a half day or one full day. About half of the workers (50.9 per cent) drew unemployment benefit at some time during the year; the average amount drawn by these workers was 92 days but only a small proportion of workers were registered as unemployed for the whole of any week for which they drew benefit.

After considering these statistics, and other specially collected for them,[19] the committee was able to record the agreed view that unemployment insurance was operating unsatisfactorily in the industry:

> Among all sections within the industry there has been general agreement that the present application of the Unemployment Insurance Scheme in the case of port transport workers is unsatisfactory. The view is commonly held that the whole structure of the Scheme is upon an unsuitable basis for dealing with the particular problem of unemployment.[20]

However, the remedies proposed to deal with the unsatisfactory operation of the unemployment insurance scheme differed considerably.

> The National Council of Port Labour Employers ... suggested that a reduction in the present expenditure should be brought about by the return of the whole Scheme to a strict actuarial basis, and that special provision should be made to deal with those who exploit the Scheme and those who though casually employed are in receipt of reasonable wages. They regard it as fundamentally wrong that men who are largely in regular employment or are earning high wages should be legally entitled to qualify for unemployment benefit for any of the days which they are idle.[21]

The Transport and General Workers' Union took a completely different approach to the question:

> On the other hand, the Transport and General Workers' Union, while equally emphatic about the unsatisfactory features of the existing provisions, regard it as impossible to provide satisfactorily for the peculiar problem of under-employment in a Scheme which was based upon the conception of unemployment in general ... They expressed the view that the Scheme is entirely adequate and does not afford the correct method of distributing unemployment benefit if it is to assist decasualisation. The union contended that more satisfactory provision could be made through a special scheme.[22]

The scheme proposed was for a guaranteed weekly wage of 50 shillings a week as well as retirement pensions (supplementary to the state old age pension and paid at the rate of 25 shillings a week provided a worker had at least 15 years of service). This scheme would be funded by the current unemployment insurance contributions of employers, employees and the state, which would be transferred from the Unemployment Insurance Fund, a sum paid by the state equal to the current deficit on the Unemployment Insurance Fund as far as the dockers were concerned, and a levy on all goods and passengers using the ports.

The chairman of the committee had attempted to mediate between the union and employers' views on registration, but on the question of unemployment insurance he was less direct. He simply recorded the need for 'drastic changes' and suggested that the subject should be examined in detail by the Royal Commission on Unemployment Insurance which had been established.[23]

The Committee, then, despite their recognition of the problem areas, failed to agree on specific measures to deal with the issues of registration and unemployment insurance. However, there was one matter on which members of the committee were able to agree on a specific recommendation; this was that a new Standing Advisory Committee should be established by the National Joint Council for Dock Labour (but with the assistance of a Ministry of Labour secretariat). The committee would have the job of encouraging and reviewing the progress on registration and decasualisation in the industry.

The Royal Commission on Unemployment

The Royal Commission on Unemployment had been established and sat while the Maclean Committee was considering the issues of registration and maintenance. The Royal Commission had a wider remit than the Maclean Committee: its terms of reference asked it to inquire into the working of the Unemployment Insurance Scheme as it affected the whole of British industry, rather than just th* port transport industry. Nevertheless, there was some overlap between the interests of the two inquiries and this overlap, as has been noted, was referred to in the report of the Maclean Committee. The Chairman of the Maclean Committee expressed the hope that the Commission might be able to resolve the disagreement between the employers and unions over the issue of maintenance.

In many ways the Commission's report, in particular as far as it affected dockers, was a disappointment. It reviewed the evidence presented by both sides of industry, evidence which did little more than confirm the position adopted before the Maclean Committee. It dismissed the Transport and General Workers' Union's argument for a special maintenance scheme for the industry.

> In our view, a special scheme involving so great an additional charge on the Exchequer could not be recommended.[24]

However, it argued that dockers should continue to be covered by the general Unemployment Insurance Scheme. It suggested that two of the amendments it was proposing to the general scheme would help to curtail some of the abuses that the employers had pointed to. One of these was that the weekly earnings of claimants who earned more that £1 a week should be taken into account when assessing benefit. Another was that steps should be taken to try to ensure that people ho claimed unemployment benefit had not turned down suitable work. These recommendations clearly came closer to the views expressed by the Transport and General Workers' Union. In practice, though, neither side was entirely happy and many employers felt that the recommendations were not strong enough.

The Unemployment Insurance Act 1934

The specific issue of decasualisation was considered by the Commission and touched upon in their report. The Commission accepted that Government action might have to be taken to help to regularise employment on the docks but expressed a clear preference for voluntary action. When the Unemployment Insurance Act was passed in 1934 clause 28 dealt directly with this matter and could have been interpreted as an indication that the Government had taken the view that the time was right for them to intervene. Clause 28 said:

> Where any scheme for regularity of employment in any industry is approved by the Minister, the Minister may in accordance with arrangements made by him with the consent of the Treasury, assist the administration of the scheme by attaching officers of the Ministry of Labour to helping the administration thereof and by such other means as he thinks fit. The Minister may in accordance with such arrangement as aforesaid, issue on behalf of employers to persons to whom such scheme applies, sums by way of wages or additional benefits in espect of unemployment or compensation for loss of employment.[25]

In fact, the Government did not use the clause to enable them to encourage schemes which would help to regularise employment; they simply used it to enable them to continue the well established practice of offering to assist with the administration of any schemes that were set up. It was also made known that the powers given to the Minister in this clause to issue money to support schemes for regularisation of employment would only be used if it was understood that later he would be reimbursed.

The Standing Advisory Committee

Both the Maclean Committee and the Royal Commission on Unemployment Insurance were a disappointment to those who wanted to see moves made to eventually eliminate the use of casual employment on the docks. However, one of the recommendations of the Maclean Committee was acted upon and had a substantial impact on the moves to establish registration and maintenance schemes; this was the recommendation that the National Joint Council for the Port Transport Industry set up a Standing Advisory Committee. The Committee was established in 1931 with equal numbers of representatives from both sides of industry and with Sir Alfred Booth and Ernest Bevin as joint chairman. The objects of the committee were:

1.   The establishment and development of joint registration schemes in all ports.

2.   The systematic and regular review of registers and arrangements for regular consideration of employment records.

3.   Provision for the recruitment of labour.

4.   The establishment of uniform methods of compiling statistics from all ports, and the collection of information showing accurately the progress of decasualisation in the industry as a whole. Representations to the Ministry of Labour, with the object of securing accurate official statistics relating to the industry.

5.   The establishment and development of systems of control or surplus stands or other means of securing the best use of available registered labour in all ports, in accordance with local needs.

6.   Detailed observations of the operation of schemes with the object of making local experience available for general use.[26]

The first meeting of the committee was held in September of 1931 and four area sub-committees were set up to review and monitor developments in different parts of the country.

Over the following 6 years or so the Standing Advisory Committee assisted in establishing and refining registration schemes in a number of ports. This work was steady if unspectacular. No major breakthroughs were achieved but consolidation and minor improvement was reported. The Committee, for example, was able to go some way towards securing better statistical information on employment at the ports. Thus, by 1938, the National Secretary of the Transport and General Workers' Union docks group was able to report to his members:

The Standing Advisory Committee ... has been responsible for assisting in investigating and securing statistical information which is of incalculable value.[27]

The Committee was also able to help get central call stands and surplus stands established at a number of ports; for instance in 1936 a central call stand was erected at Grimsby which permitted the engagement of all labour under one roof. The Ministry of Labour was persuaded to accept that they should assist in the provision of similar buildings at Bristol, Middlesborough and Preston. Further, the Committee was able to persuade employers and dockers at some of the ports which did not have registration schemes to adopt one, and in other cases where registration schemes were already in operation at the ports the Committee played a useful role in revising the schemes and bringing them into line with the practice at the best regulated ports, particularly over the revision and the control of the size of the register.

Wages Dispute and Decasualisation

Early in 1937 the Transport and General Workers' Union began formulating a new wage demand for the port transport industry. In part, the impetus behind such a demand was the improvement in general economic conditions. However, a justification for the wage demand was that dockers were underemployed and therefore needed to be compensated through higher wages. The employers resisted the wage demand, but they did so not by totally rejecting the argument put forward by the unions; rather they suggested that higher wages would not solve the real problem. Their reply to the wage demand, then, was to argue that moves needed to be made to deal with the unde employment in the industry, through a measure of decasualisation. Thus, they said:

It is frankly admitted that overseas shipping is enjoying better times (although this statement hardly applies to coastwise shipping), but the employers feel that such additional expenditure as they are prepared to incur should be devoted to a further and determined joint attack upon the problem of decasualisation within the industry. By this means and by better regularisation of the labour force, it should be possible to increase the general level of earnings of the men and consequently improve their standard of life, which is, after all, the desired end which both sides have so much at heart.[28]

The employers specific proposals called for the recognition of three different classes of dock worker. The first, "A" class men, would be guaranteed 20 days work a month at time rate provided they were available for work. The second group, "B" class men, would be given preference for work after the "A" class men had been placed. It was suggested that a joint approach might be made to the Ministry of Labour to see what contribution the Government might make from the Unemployment Fund towards establishing a guaranteed weekly wage for these men (the assumption was that the guarantee would be slightly lower than that offered to "A" class men). The third group "C" class men would be casual workers who would provide the necessary reserve of labour for the industry. Thus it was stated by the employers in their proposal:

It may always be necessary for the industry to have some fringe of "casual" men. It is not practicable to cover these with any guar ntee or by any other means, but it is proposed that from this class recruits, if suitable, to "B" and then "A" classes will be drawn.[29]

The employers' proposals clearly put the Transport and General Workers' Union in a difficult position. There was a suspicion that the employers were simply making their proposals on decasualisation in order to deflect attention from the wage claim; yet the employers' proposals were far more detailed and showed a willingness to consider a much more extensive degree of decasualisation than ever before. The importance attached to decasualisation by the Transport and General Workers' Union meant that the offer could not easily be ignored. Ernest Bevin, when he reported to the union on his discussions with the employers said:

I took the line that while I had been struggling for over a quarter of a century (to get decasualisation), I could not regard the employers' statement as a satisfactory answer to the wage claim .... The question of security as against casual labour on the docks, however, is a very important matter, and on reflection, I am convinced that the proposal, if worked out to a logical conclusion, cannot be lightly thrown away.[30]

The agreement eventually reached provided for a wage increase of one shilling a day and included a clause committing both sides to further decasualisation as a matter of urgency. Thus, it said:

The parties shall confer jointly forthwith, both nationally and locally, in order to give effect to a scheme for the greatest possible measure of decasualisation of labour in the ports.[31]

Discussion over decasualisation took place between 1937 and the beginning of the Second World War. Two issues held up progress. One was the size of the dock labour force. The employers argued that the size of the registered labour force had to be reduced if maintenance was to be a practical proposition. The unions were not unwilling to see such reductions, and in fact had argued in favour of such action in the past, but they were aware of the resistance to such moves in many ports. The second, and in some ways much more crucial issue, was that of the cost of any scheme of maintenance. The employers argued that Government financial

57

assistance was essential before any scheme could be devised. Such assistance might be given under the terms of the 1934 Unemployment Insurance Act. Of course, this line of argument was consistent with the proposals on decasualisation put forward during the 1937 wages dispute; in those proposals they had made it clear that a guaranteed week could only be provided for what they termed "B" class men, if Government financial assistance was forthcoming. Throughout 1938 Bevin reported to the Transport and General Workers' Union on the negotiations with the employers in optimistic terms.[32] However, he recognised that an agreement would be impossible without a Government grant (he said that "a solution of the problem was dependent upon the receipt of a Government grant for a period of at least 10 years in lieu of the present Unemployment Benefit").[33] In the end the Government rejected the appeal for financial assistance on the grounds that the amount needed was likely to be well in excess of that suggested by the employers and if granted was likely to be used as a precedent for other industries.

Transport and General Workers' Union's Commitment to Decasualisation

The history of the moves to deal with the problems arising from the use of the casual system of employment on the docks from 1922 to 1939, as has been illustrated, was one of constant pressure from the Transport and General Workers' Union; pressure on both the employers and different governments. If by the beginning of the Second World War relatively little seemed to have been achieved, this was the result of the unfavourable economic conditions and at first the resistance and then the uncertain reaction of governments and employers to moves towards decasualisation more than anything else; it certainly was not the result of any lack of enthusiasm on the part of the Transport and General Workers' Union.

The Transport and General Workers' Union's enthusiasm for moves towards decasualisation, and the importance they attached to such moves can be shown not simply by reference to the pressure they put on the employers and government on such matters but also by reference by their public and private statements. For example, in their evidence to the 1930 Maclean Committee the Transport and General Workers' Union's representatives said:

> The industry is so peculiar in character that it cannot be likened to any other class of employment. Men are in continual attendance for work, and are expected to be ready to answer any call made by the employers without warning. This makes it imperative that there should be some comprehensive scheme in the case of dock workers for dealing with both employment and unemployment together as one problem.[34]

In this memorandum the union made it clear that they did not consider registration alone an answer to the problem, though as they had made argued on other occasions they recognised registration to be valuable; in one public statement, Bevin claimed that he was close to being "the father of registration" and said that "he wanted to see it in every port" because he "saw no other way of getting the docker an industrial status".[35] A solution to the problem of casual labour, however, had to go beyond registration, and include the provision of maintenance.

Possibly more convincing than such public statements are the private ones. References to decasualisation, registration and maintenance occur on numerous occasions throughout records of meetings of the Transport and General Workers' Union National Executive Council, and the Docks Group. Time and time again the union's officers stressed the importance of these matters.

For example, in 1925, it was stated that:

The largest problem confronting us at the moment is that of registration.[36]

It was emphasised that the officers would continue their efforts to get registration schemes adopted in all ports as one way of alleviating the problems arising from casual employment, or what was referred to as "the evil conditions" and "this vexed social problem".[37] Two years later the National Conference of the Union approved a resolution stating that schemes of registration should be adopted in all ports. The following year in a debate in the Scottish Area Committee about a ballot in Aberdeen over registration, it was noted that "registration was the recognised policy of the Union' and argued that 'the Docks' Secretary was quite within his rights in using expressions to indicate his own convictions on the subject".[38] In 1930, it was reported that the National Delegate Conference of the Dock Group had been "magnificent ... from all points of view" and had adopted "bold proposals on decasualisation".[39] In 1938, Bevin, reporting on discussions on decasualisation with the employers said:

> I am firmly convinced that if a (decasualisation) scheme could be established it would be one of the greatest strokes that has ever been done for the Docks Industry ...[40]

One strand in the explanation that can be given for the Transport and General Workers' Union's position in relation to registration and maintenance is clear from the above discussion; casual employment had socially and economically undesirable consequences and moves to eradicate casual work would be one of the most important ways of improving the conditions of the dock labourer. There is, however, another strand; that is, the Transport and General Workers' Union saw registration in particular as a way of increasing its own power in the docks and establishing itself as the only union to represent dockers. Thus it has been argued:

> The secretary of the Transport and General Workers' Union, Ernest Bevin, consistently sought to bring all port workers within the embrace of the amalgamation, and saw registration as essential to the success of this policy. His union asserted a sole right to discuss this issue with employers and government at national level and it was prepared, on occasion, to exploit its powerful position on local port labour committees to oust smaller rivals from the waterside.[41]

Bean has noted how the Transport and General Workers' Union in the port of Liverpool used registration as a means of boosting a flagging membership in the early 1920s. He pointed out that figures from October 1923 suggested out of 15,000 men working regularly in the docks only between 10,000 and 12,000 were paying subscriptions even though at one time they had probably all been in good standing. Moreover, the union's efforts to use registration as a way of boosting membership were supported by the employers because they saw the union as having a role to play in controlling the workforce.

Employers were also aware that if they wished the union to be in a position to control its members and deliver a disciplined workforce, then to retain credibility as a representative body its organisational strength had to be preserved. The fact was, however, that during the 1920s the union had been faced with a serious loss of subscribing membership. Consequently, although they continued to oppose the principle of compulsory union membership and were determined not to allow the docks to b come a "closed preserve from the present dockers and their sons", employers were prepared to accede to the union's request for a re-registration of tally holders as a means of restoring its membership sanction for the union in that pressure could be put on men to rejoin because applications required endorsement by the union or employer, and preferably both.[42]

The corollary is that the other smaller unions, who the Transport and General Workers' Union was trying to displace, had every reason to be cautious, and ultimately to oppose the introduction of registration. The National Amalgamated Stevedores and Dockers, for example, reconstituted in 1927, though in existence as a separate organisation before, opposed registration schemes in London and Hull when it was excluded from a controlling interest in them, and, throughout the interwar years, found itself championing those who were suspicious of the moves towards registration.

It is difficult, if not impossible, to distinguish the varying strengths of these motivating forces for the position adopted by the Transport and General Workers' Union. Clearly registration was one way in which the union could increase its control over the industry, and its attempts to exclude other unions from participation in such schemes is testimony to the importance it attached to this move. The union only supported registration when it had at least joint control of the registration process. It always sought to exclude other unions and to extend its power. Yet to deny that there was a genuine belief in the value of registration for the docker would also be a mistake. Increasingly concern on this matter became critical for union officials.

Memberships Reactions to Registration and Maintenance

It would be wrong to claim or give the impression that only Bevin or only senior officers in the Transport and General Workers' Union were in favour of pressing for the introduction of schemes of registration and maintenance. It has been noted already that at one point one area committee complained that insufficient progress was being made on registration and that the National Executive Council had to argue that progress was as swift as might reasonably be expected in the circumstances. On a number of other occasions Bevin, in particular, took the issues of registration and maintenance to delegate conferences of dockers and received firm backing for the moves he was making. Similarly in 1930, the officers committee of the Transport and General Workers' Union was able to report that it had distributed its draft scheme for registration and maintenance to branches, and the scheme had been welcomed, "there having been no criticism or complaint with regard to the same".[43] The national docks secretary, Milford, was able to claim in 1935[44] that union membership on the docks had increased and implied that this indicated satisfaction with union policy in this area. In fact, in this particular instance, one has to be a little sceptical of the interpretation placed on these figures, for, in the period he referred to, union membership generally was beginning to increase from the depths of the depression,[45] and many of the registration agreements concluded at this time, if they did not provide for a closed shop (and some of them did), at least enabled the union to identify potential members better and to put pressure on them to join. Nevertheless, the general point, that support for registration and maintenance was not limited to senior officers stands.

However, at the same time it needs to be recognised that despite support for registration and maintenance in some sections of the union, there was also opposition to it in others. Possibly the most serious opposition was felt in a number of the ports which resisted attempts to set up registration schemes or abandon them once they had been established. The classic case in this context is provided by the port of Glasgow.

There was a long history of opposition to registration at Glasgow. Earlier the successful opposition to registration in 1912 was reported. Although a scheme operated on a temporary basis towards the end of the First World War, it was eventually rejected by dock workers after the War. Similarly, a registration scheme prepared at the suggestion of the Ministry of Labour in 1923 was rejected, and although following the interim reports of the Maclean Committee another scheme was prepared and recommended for acceptance by union officials, after a deputation from the union at Glasgow visited Liverpool to see how registration was operating there, and reported adversely on it, the proposed scheme was rejected. The Docks Group minutes record the anger of officials and how they blamed the 'prejudice' of the Glasgow leaders:

> ... and a Deputation was appointed to go to Liverpool. The Deputation reported back to a General meeting and reported against the adoption of Registration in Glasgow. They introduced matters in regard to working conditions which had nothing whatever to do with Registration. Their report was full of prejudice and the men turned the scheme down.[46]

The opposition of the Glasgow branch to decasualisation brought them into conflict with the national policy of the Transport and General Workers' Union, particularly from 1927 onwards. In that year the union's delegate conference had passed a resolution calling for registration schemes to be adopted in all ports. The reaction of the Glasgow branch was to form themselves into the "Anti-Registration League" and so to determine to resist any attempt to introduce registration at Glasgow. However, the opposition of the Glasgow branch to registration and their conflict with the national union was mixed with conflict over other items. One of these also came to head at the 1927 delegate conference of the union. At that conference it was decided that entry to the union should be available to all dockers, with a maximum entrance fee of £5.

This decision was opposed by the Glasgow branch because many dockers wanted to exclude from membership men who worked for the Clyde Trust who had supported an earlier national strike. At a branch meeting on 4 September 1927, the Glasgow dockers determined to oppose both conference decisions, and warned that they were "determined to resist them, no matter what the consequences may be, even to secede from the union".[47] This brought a reply from Bevin that the decision on the maximum entrance fee had been made by 'the supreme governing body of the Union, viz, the second Biennial Delegate Conference' and the Executive had no intention of departing from it. Bevin went on to refer to the issue of registration which had been mentioned in the Glasgow resolution (it had referred to the Executive Committee "insisting" on Registration). He said that the National Executive had never tried to impose registration on Glasgow, but had merely referred the matter to the trade group.[48]

In practice, though, the Executive Council of the Transport and General Workers' Union accepted that for the time being there was little they could do to press the issue of registration. Bevin had reported to the Executive that, in his view, there was "no possibility of the Glasgow Dock members ever agreeing to the principle of Registration,"[49] and therefore the Council decided to concentrate on the issue of union membership. In late September 1927 they passed a resolution in effect indicating that they were not going to take any action over registration themselves:

> The problem of Registration in its application to dock employment in the Port of Glasgow is a matter for the attention of the National Committee of the Docks Group.[50]

In November of the same year, however, they passed another resolution indicating that they were concerned centrally with the issue of union membership.

(1)   That the executive express their view that ... they desire that these men of the Clyde Trust should be given a badge ...

(2)   They are desirous that men who are working and getting their living on the Docks and who are not members, who can show that they have been working regular for a considerable period and ought to be contributing to the union, to be enrolled in the branches[51]

Despite the decision of the Transport and General Workers' Union's Executive Council, the Glasgow branch refused to admit the employees of the Clyde Trust or other dockers to membership and the branch committee resigned rather than carry out the Executive Council's decision. A number of attempts were made to resolve the problem early in 1928, but without success, and, in May 1928, Bevin recommended to the Union's General Executive Council that matters should be allowed to rest for a while.

During the past few months a great deal of mischief has been attempted by the recalcitrant members and I had to seriously consider taking drastic steps to deal with the position. However, time is a great healer, and on reflection, I decided that it would be better to allow a further opportunity for the position to work itself out.[52]

This approach appeared to work, for later in 1928 a sub-committee of the Executive was able to visit Glasgow and reach an agreement with the Glasgow branch which allowed limited new entry to the union, and the agreement was endorsed by a mass meeting of the dockers. However, in January 1929, a meeting of Glasgow dockers refused to allow the Clyde Trust men to join the union. The Area minutes of the union record that "at the Glasgow Docks meeting held on Sunday, the 22nd of January, 85 voted in favour of accepting the ictimised Clyde Trust men, and 129 voted against their acceptance."[53]

The question of registration also resurfaced again in 1929. On this occasion it was first raised by the employers in the port. The local agreement covering the port was terminated by the union in April 1929 and, during the course of negotiations on a new agreement, the employers proposed that the issue of registration should be given priority. The Executive Council of the Transport and General Workers' Union was placed in a difficult position. They were on record as favouring registration, and many of them, like Bevin, had fought for many years to have registration schemes established in all ports. Further, at the national level, they had been arguing for registration schemes to be established on a comprehensive basis as part of a scheme for maintenance. However, at the same time, they knew that any attempt to press for registration would be opposed by their members in Glasgow.

Initially, the Executive Council tried to sidestep the issue by stating that while it was in favour of registration it was not willing to see it used as a precondition for other negotiations. Thus, in a resolution passed at a meeting held on 3 April 1930, they said:

That in view of the fact that the Glasgow Dock Section is opposed to the principle of registration at the present time, and the further fact that registration is not obligatory under the National Docks Agreement, this committee is not prepared to accept a position which mak s the re-establishment of a local agreement conditional upon the acceptance of the principle of registration.[54]

However, this attempt to avoid conflict between the General Executive Council of the union and the Glasgow branch failed. The discussion of registration had been re-started and the dockers at Glasgow were afraid that they were going to be forced into a registration scheme as a result of the combined efforts of the employers and the union's national officers. In March 1930 the Glasgow branch passed a resolution which said:

> It is the opinion of this meeting that, despite the well-meant promotion in the first instance of dockers' registration by amateur social reformers, dockers registration is not, and cannot be, a step towards the solution of the problem of poverty associated with the general under-employment of casual dock labour, and that where registration is in operation, notably in Liverpool, it has increased rather than diminished the general under-employment. It is also our opinion that from the Employers' point of view registration has long since resolved itself into a mere instrument of discipline and coercion, and that from the point of view of our Trade Union officials, who are its assiduous promoters, as borne out by the Minutes of our Meetings with the Employers, registration provides a solution of their vexed problem of stabilizing the Union amongst Glasgow dockers, and therefore of providing themselves with the maximum security in the undisturbed enjoyment of their salaries and superannuation. The proposed maintenance scheme we regard as only a palpable bait to involve us in the toils of the slavery of registration.[55]

At the Maclean Committee representatives of the Glasgow dockers gave evidence, to the embarrassment of the Transport and General Workers' national officials. The conflict which the Executive Council had sought to side-step was brought out into the open and there was fierce debate at the Maclean committee hearings between the national and Glasgow dockers' representatives.[56]

It is important, at this juncture to note another source of conflict between the national officials of the Transport and General Workers' Union and the Glasgow dockers; this was the issue of the appointment of local officials. When the Scottish Union of Dock Workers amalgamated with the Transport and General Workers' Union (the membership only agreed to the amalgamation after a second ballot) discussions took place, during which, the Glasgow branch claimed, an assurance was given that they would be able to appoint their own fulltime officials. In fact, the executive council of the Transport and General Workers' Union refused the Glasgow branch the right to appoint their officials, stating that this would be contrary to the general policy that all fulltime officials should be appointed at the centre, and the Glasgow branches claim about assurances they had been given was challenged by the Area officials. Nevertheless, the Glasgow branch continued to press for the right to appoint their own officials and for them to be subject to periodic re-election. A dispute arose over the appointment of a docks delegate in 1924 and the following year a General Meeting passed a resolution expressing determination 'to exercise its constitutional rights to annually elect its own Branch Officers, including the Branch Secretary, Branch Delegates, Branch Committee, Officers in Sub-offices, Branch Chairmen and Branch Auditors'. The resolution went on to complain about the "irregular, high-handed and unconstitutional" action of the National Executive Council.[58] Two years later they tried to get a resolution passed at the 1927 Biennial Delegate Conference of the union to allow them to appoint their own officials, but the resolution was defeated. Subsequently the Glasgow branch took the matter to court and won, but the National Executive Council continued to resist the idea, and said that they would try to have the rules of the union changed at the next Biennial Delegate Conference so that the court decision could be reversed. In the meantime the Glasgow branch appointed their own officials. When the rules of the Transport and General Workers' Union were changed the National Executive Council agreed to recognise all officials still in post but attempted to assert their right to appoint future officials. Meetings held to discuss the issue failed to find a compromise acceptable to both sides, so that by 1931 effectively an impasse had been reached.

In 1932 the Glasgow branch broke away from the Transport and General Workers' Union to form the Scottish Transport and General Workers' Union. They were joined by dockers from Grangemouth; the Assistant General Secretary of the Transport and General Workers' Union accepted that the "Breakaway Union succeeded to a considerable extent in Grangemouth; practically all the men in the casual section on the registers enrolled themselves in the Breakaway Union". Later, however, he contended that the Area Committee and the Union were sure that "we shall hold Grangemouth and before much time passes we shall drive the new union out of Grangemouth".[59] The Area Union minutes record that in May 1932 "a large number of the men were sitting on the fence and not paying to any union", but also was confident that "within a week or two the position at Grangemouth would be retrieved".[60] In October of the same year, it was reported that the "breakaway union in Grangemouth had been practically exterminated"[61], with only 30 men not having returned to the Transport and General Workers' Union. Initially, dockers at Leith also joined the breakaway, though not to the same extent as in Grangemouth.

Undoubtedly, despite the extension of the breakaway to some other ports, the centre of attention and the centre of the conflict within the Union was at Glasgow. Further, although the dispute over the appointment of officers was the catalyst for the move to set up the union, it was by no means the only factor behind the breakaway. The decision to secede from the Transport and General Workers' Union was the culmination of nearly a decade of disagreement and dispute between the Glasgow branch and the central union. One part of this was the disagreement over registration and maintenance. Essentially, the Glasgow dockers wanted to control their own affairs and to retain their own ways of doing things; this applied whether the item under discussion was the appointment of officials, the entry of new members, or registration and maintenance.

The importance to the registration issue in th breakaway movement at Glasgow was stressed by an official inquiry which examined the events some five years later. It said:

> The evidence shows that the breakaway of the Glasgow dockers from the Transport and General Workers' Union, though the immediate occasion of it was a controversy on another matter, was in a large measure brought about by the difference that had arisen between them as to the policy to be adapted with regard to registration.[62]

Further support for this assessment can be gained from events after the formation of the Scottish Transport and General Workers' Union. Even with their own union the Glasgow dockers continued to resist registration. They abandoned the Anti-Registration League but the officials of the League became the officers of the new union and pursued the same policies. In 1936 a further attempt was made to introduce greater regularity of working on the docks at Glasgow[63] but this was rejected by the union and its members.

The disagreement over registration between the membership at Glasgow and the central union is probably the best illustration of membership discontent over the policy of the Transport and General Workers' Union on registration and maintenance. Nevertheless, examples can also be given from other ports. In one of the other Scottish ports, Aberdeen, for instance, the registration scheme broke down in the late 1920s and for a number of years neither workers nor employers eriously sought to introduce a new scheme. However, in November 1933 the employers accepted advice from the Standing Advisory Committee and proposed a new scheme, based on the national model. The union branch rejected the scheme despite a threat that if the scheme were rejected the Government might take steps to enforce their own. In fact the statement "was regarded by the members of the union as a "threat" and seems to have strengthened their antagonism to registration."[64]   Anyway, the threat was an idle one for the Government had no power and showed no inclination to enforce a scheme of their own.

Aberdeen's failure to introduce a new registration led the National Joint Council for Dock Labour to ask the Minister of Labour to appoint a Board of Inquiry to examine the position at the port.[65]   The Board was established in 1937 with J M Irvine as its chairman. The board was faced immediately with the opposition of dockers at Aberdeen not simply to registration but also to their inquiry. The Aberdeen dockers' branch of the Transport and General Workers' Union refused to give evidence to the Board because they believed that it was simply a device to impose registration on them. The national union had to ask one of its national officers to attend the inquiry on the union's behalf, although later the local branch relaxed its earlier total opposition to the inquiry and allowed its secretary to give evidence.

According to the Board of Inquiry the members of the union at Aberdeen did not oppose the objectives of registration (the regulation of employment), but they argued the method of hiring labour then in operation in Aberdeen, by which preference was given to union members (who had proof of such membership through a badge renewed quarterly), achieved the same objectives. The overall issue, and the reason for the Aberdeen dockers' refusal to accept a registration scheme, was that under such a scheme they would have to give up control over entry to a joint committee.

> The objections stated by the members of the Union to the proposals contained in that (registration) scheme closely resembled those stated by the Glasgow dockers ... They consider it to be initially important that the existing rights of the Union won by the trade union organisation and long established in the port, should be maintained, and they refused to surrender to a joint committee functions and powers now exercised by the Union or to assent to any proposals which would have the effect of giving the Employers' Association an equal voice with the Union in the exercise of those functions and powers. The members of the Union are resolutely opposed to the proposal to introduce employment record books in substitution for the Union badge as the token for preference. They contend that, under existing conditions at Aberdeen, the use of employment record books, used in the manner and for the purpose set out in the scheme of 29th November, 1933, as part and parcel of a machinery designed to bring the workers under a system of rigid supervision and control, which would restrict the freedom of choice which they now have in their search for work suitable to their individual skill and experience and would be in the nature of "industrial conscription[65]

The Board suggested that a compromise might be reached between the views of the dockers and the views of the national union and employers' representatives. Their compromise was based on a continued use of the current system of allocating work, with special measures being introduced to enable the collection of essential employment data, and the erection of central call stands. The compromise was rejected by the employers on the advice of the national union and employers' representatives.

In a number of other Scottish ports the position was mirrored. Problems were encountered persuading dockers in Dundee, Grangemouth, Bo'ness and Leith to accept registration schemes. In some cases they explicitly followed the lead of the larger ports. One review by the Union of the problems of introducing registration schemes in Scottish ports drew particular attention to the opposition of many dockers.

> Discussions took place as to the enforcement of the Scheme in every Port, but it was explained that while in London the employers were principally to blame for the

non-operation of the Scheme, in Scotland it was, in some cases, the men who were responsible for the delay.[67]

In other ports, like London and Hull, local opposition to registration was not effective for such a long period, but in the case of Hull it prevented the establishment of a scheme after the First World War until 1925, and even later local opposition kept causing difficulties and disputes. In the case of London the position was complicated by, as has already been mentioned, the operations of the Amalgamated Stevedores Protection League (later to become the National Amalgamated Stevedores and Dockers) and the attempted breakaway led by Thomson and Potter, who had opposed Bevin over the 1 23 wages reduction and in 1926 tried to set up the National Union of Transport and Allied Workers. The Thomson and Potter breakaway was quickly defeated but the Stevedores Union remained to become a major opponent of the Transport and General Workers' Union.

In some ports registration schemes encountered opposition not simply because dockers were opposed to the schemes as such, but because many of the schemes included provision for disciplinary penalties against dockers who infringed regulations. In a number of cases the opposition to the use of disciplinary penalties led to strike action; for example, at Salford in 1934.

Two strikes occurred in Salford towards the end of 1934. In October two thousand men went on strike because the Manchester Ship Canal Company dismissed three men who had been expelled from the union for taking part in a previous unofficial strike. As a report written at the time made clear, the "strikers'' grievance was not against the Ship Canal Company, but against the Transport and General Workers' Union.[68] That particular strike was quickly settled but conflict returned to the port in the following month.[69] This time the issue was overtime working. 120 men ignored an instruction from the Ship Canal Company and were suspended from work. Other dockers went on unofficial strike only returning when the company declared its intention of bringing in substitute labour.

The extent of opposition to registration and maintenance amongst dockers in the inter-war years was recognised by one of Bevin's biographers, Bullock, who argued that Bevin never convinced some dockers of the need to accept that the casual system of employment should be changed.

> Dock work (in the inter-war years) had still a highly personal element in it. A docker stayed with a particular firm or preferred to work for a particular foreman, often valued highly the freedom to work or not to work as he felt inclined and lived in a closed world in which son frequently succeeded father on both sides of the industry, the history of port disputes was handed down and a intricate set of customs governed every operation. Bevin's drive for decasualisation brought him into conflict with this closed world of which casual labour was the inherited way of life. The argument that they would be better off under a different system did not convince, and to some extent has still not convinced many dockers who clung to the old ways.[70]

It is fair to point out, however, that in fact Bevin recognised that he faced strong opposition from within the membership of his own union. On a number of occasions he complained within the union about 'the obstinacy of some of our own people'[71] and in one report to the General Council he argued that maintenance was being held up as much by their own members as anything else.

> The delay that has taken place in the introduction of maintenance is, I am sorry to say, as much due to our side as to the Employers' side. The difficulties and prejudices to be

overcome amongst our own class are very formidable - it is really heart breaking when you cannot get your own people to fully appreciate the efforts the union is making to protect their life and labour.[72]

Nevertheless, despite the fact that Bevin recognised the opposition from within the membership to schemes of registration and maintenance he did not allow this to deflect him from supporting such schemes and from trying to get them adopted in all British ports. In Bevin's eyes the opposition was misplaced and had to be overcome rather than met.

Notes

1. Court of Inquiry into Transport Workers.
2. Transport and General Workers' Union General Executive Council Minutes, 11 February 1924, p32.
3. Clause 9 of the agreement signed on 20 February 1924.
4. Great Yarmouth.
5. Dock Transport Workers (Registration and Guaranteed Week Committee), First Interim Report, London, 1924, para.4.
6. Dock Transport Workers (Registration and Guaranteed Week Committee), Second Interim Report, London, 1924, paras.3, 4.
7. Area No.6.
8. Transport and General Workers' Union General Executive Council Minutes, 18 February 1925, p16, minute 93.
9. Port Labour Inquiry, HMSO, London, 1930, Summary of Special Reports from Joint Registration Committees, July 1930, p3.
10. *Ibid*, p9.
11. Transport and General Workers' Union Annual Report, 1927, p26.
12. Memorandum on Maintenance, prepared for the Maclean Committee on Decasualisation of Dock Labour, issued on 20 February 1926 by E Bevin.
13. Blanesburgh Committee.
14. Transport and General Workers' Union Annual Report, 1928, p24.
15. Port Labour Inquiry, *Op Cit*, p49.
16. *Ibid*, p5.
17. *Ibid*, pp16-17.
18. *Ibid*, p43.
19. They received reports from all port registration committees and detailed statistics from a number of them. They were also aware of a report by F G Hanham into the workings of the Unemployment Insurance Scheme on the Liverpool docks.
20. Port Labour Inquiry, *OP Cit*, p59.
21. *Ibid*, p59.
22. *Ibid*, pp59-60.
23. Royal Commission on Unemployment Insurance, *Report* HMSO, London, 1932.
24. *Ibid*, p245.
25. Unemployment Insurance Act, 934, clause 28.
26. Transport and General Workers' Union Annual Reports, 1931/33, p67.
27. Transport and General Workers' Union Annual Reports, 1937/8, p67.
28. Reply dated 6 August 1937, quoted in Transport and General Workers' Union Annual Report, 1937, p276.

29.   *Ibid,* p276.

30.   Transport and General Workers' Union General Secretary's Report to General Executive Council, 16 August 1937, p272.

31.   Quoted from the agreement.

32.   See for example reports of Bevin to Transport and General Workers' Union General Executive Council on 7 March 1938 and 9 March 1938.

33.   Transport and General Workers' Union General Executive Council Minutes 9, March 1938, p70, minute 228.

34.   Evidence submitted by the Port Labour Inquiry, 1930 by the Transport and General Workers' Union, in the report of the Inquiry, *Op Cit,* p65.

35.   Eastern Morning News, 26 November 1923.

36.   General Secretary's Report to the Transport and General Workers' Union General Executive Council, 5 June 1925, p40.

37.   General Secretary's Report to the Transport and General Workers' Union General Executive Council, 31 December 1925, p23.

38.   Transport and General Workers' Union, Scottish Area Minutes, 17 June 1928, Minute 17.

39.   General Secretary's Report to the Transport and General Workers' Union General Executive Council, 17 November 1930, p252.

40.   General Secretary's Report to the Transport and General Workers' Union General Executive Council, 7 March 1938, p57.

41.   G Phillips, N Whiteside, *Casual Employment,* Clarendon Press, Oxford, 1985, p223.

42.   R Bean, Custom, Job Regulation and Dock Labour in Liverpool, 1911-39, *International Review of Social History,* Vol XXVII, Part 3, pp287-88.

43.   Meeting held at Transport House, 22,23 October 1930.

44.   Transport and General Workers' Union Annual Reports, 1933/35, p64.

45.   Nationally union membership fell in the early 1930's (in 1930 it was 4,842,000 and in 1932 it was 4,392,000) but had started to increase by 1935 (in that year membership was 4,867,000).

46.   Transport and General Workers' Union, Docks Group Minutes, 19 June 1925, minute 191.

47.   Transport and General Workers' Union General Executive Council, 26 September 1927, p208.

48.   Letter from E Bevin to J Veitch dated 29 September 1927.

49.   General Secretary's Report to the Transport and General Workers' Union General Executive Council, 28 May 1927, p136.

50.   Transport and General Workers' Union General Executive Council Minutes, 26 September 1927, p208, minute 841.

51.   Transport and General Workers' Union General Executive Council Minutes, 16 November 1927, p251, minute 1024.

52.   General Secretary's Report to the Transport and General Workers' Union General Executive Council, 16 May 1928, p128.

53.   Transport and General Workers' Union, Scottish Area Minutes, January 1929, minute 56.

54.   Transport and General Workers' Union General Executive Council Minutes, 3 April 1930, minutes 295.

55.   Quoted in Glasgow Shipowners' and Dock Labour Employers' evidence to Port Labour Inquiry 1930, p2.

56.   Reports suggest the debate became very heated and nearly led to violence.

57.   See letter from J Houghton to J Cliff dated 11 December 1931 in which Houghton said

he was certain that 'no such concession was made by those conducting the negotiations' and memo on the Glasgow Docks Branch dated 11 December 1931 prepared by the Area Secretary, J Veitch.

58.   Memo by J Veitch dated 11 December 1931.
58.   Transport and General Workers' Union, Area Minutes, 9 May 1932, minute 59.
60.   Transport and General Workers' Union, Area Minutes, 10 May 1932, minute 149.
61.   Transport and General Workers' Union, Area Minutes, 18 October 1932, minute 148.
62.   Ministry of Labour, *Port Labour in Aberdeen and Glasgow: Report of a Board of Enquiry*, HMSO, London, 1937, p22.
63.   See Report of Board of Inquiry, *Ibid*, for details.
64.   Ibid, p43.
65.   Ibid. The Board also examined the position in Glasgow.
66.   Ibid, pp44-45.
67.   Transport and General Workers' Union, Docks Group Minutes, 19 June 1926, minute 191.
68.   Times, 31 October 1934, p11.
69.   Strike lasted from 21-24 November 1934.
70.   A Bullock, *The Life and Times of Ernest Bevin*, Vol 1, Heinemann, London, 1967, p117.
71.   Transport and General Workers' Union, General Secretary's Report to General Council.
72.   Transport and General Workers' Union, General Secretary's Report to General Council.

4 Towards the Dock Labour Scheme

Demands of the War

The Second World War, like the First, brought new constraints and new demands for the port transport industry. Before war was formally declared it was recognised that the opening of hostilities inevitably would disrupt shipping: it was also recognised that efficient communications and dock operations would be important for the war effort. Discussions were held between a number of interested parties in the early part of 1939 on these matters: Bevin, representing the Transport and General Workers' Union, played an important role.

When the War began the disruption of shipping led to a reduction in the amount of traffic using the ports and a reduction in employment opportunities for dockers. The increase in the level of unemployment amongst dockers held dangers, not simply for the dockers themselves. It meant that dockers were likely to be tempted to leave the industry, some to join the armed forces: later this could mean that there would be a shortage of dockers, a shortage which could hamper the war effort.[1] Such a fear led to attempts to stabilise employment on the docks.

However, when War broke out the most immediate concern was the ability of the ports to meet the changing demands that were likely to be made on them. It was believed by all connected with the industry that this meant that dock workers had to be willing to be more mobile and accept engagements in different parts of the port or different ports. In October 1939, following negotiations within the National Joint Council for the Port Transport Industry, a scheme was adopted for the voluntary transfer of labour from one port to another.

More generally, the early part of the war was disastrous for Britain. In 1940 major political changes took place which resulted in Churchill becoming Prime Minister and Bevin became Minister of Labour. Undoubtedly the demands of the War on their own would have led to changes being made to the method of engagement of dock workers. The combination of the demands of the War and the political developments in 1940, though, ensured that the changes in this method of engagement of dock labour would take a particular direction and would be crucial for the long-term direction of employment practices in the industry. The appointment of Bevin as Minister of Labour meant that the person most associated with moves to regularise employment on the docks through registration and maintenance schemes was put in a position where he could reasonably claim that he had to compulsorily introduce such schemes not simply because he believed that it was socially just, or in his members best interests, but also because he believed that it was essential for the war effort.

Registration and Maintenance

As Minister of Labour, Bevin moved quickly to deal with the problems of the port transport industry. His first important action in this connection was to introduce the Dock Labour (Compulsory Registration) Order in June 1940. This Order had as its aim "the regularising of port employment" and it proposed to achieve the aim by introducing a system of registration in all major ports. The registers were to be established and reviewed by port registration committees, themselves composed of representatives from both sides of industry. There were a number of important aspects of this registration scheme. First, the scheme came very close to being a national one, for while local variations were acceptable, the basic structure was determined by a "model scheme" issued by the Ministry of Labour. Second, registration was to be compulsory, not voluntary as with the inter-war schemes. Third, for the first time employers as well as employees were to be registered. The following month the Ministry of Labour appointed port labour inspectors to assist in the administration of the schemes.
      The introduction of a system of registration, in such terms, and so quickly, clearly signalled the direction in which Bevin was moving. Of course, it was the direction one would have anticipated as the result of the views he expressed before becoming Minister of Labour. Later in the year further moves were made in the same direction, this time dealing with the question of maintenance as well as registration.
      In the second half of 1940 the west coast ports faced particular problems: they had to deal with increased traffic because of the transfer of shipping from the east and south coast ports, and they were harassed by bombing attacks. Delays in dealing with cargo became a matter of national concern and in December a Cabinet committee was appointed to try to improve the position. Bevin, as Minister of Labour and as a dockers' leader, was in a unique position to offer advice and to press his own preferred scheme. As a result it was agreed to introduce a new method of employment in the west coast ports.
      The new scheme was introduced in March 1941 and initially covered the main Lancashire ports. Under the scheme dock workers were to become employees of the Ministry of Transport: control was to be exercised through a Regional Port Director, and then through a variety of port officials, including a general manager, a labour superintendent and a port labour inspector. All of these officials were to be appointed by the Minister of Transport. Current port employers were encouraged to continue in operation, but as far as relations with dock workers were concerned, on a different basis than before. They were no longer to have direct responsibility for dock workers: payment of wages was to be through the Regional Port Director and discipline was to be the responsibility of the port officials, subject to review by a joint employer/employee committee. A crucial element of the new scheme was the provision for maintenance. Dock workers were to receive a guaranteed wage of 7 shillings and 6 pence (7 shillings in the smaller ports) a half-day (based on 11 half-day shifts a week) provided they presented themselves for work regularly.
      The west coast scheme was clearly more important and a more fundamental development than the registration order introduced in June 1940. Not only did it introduce maintenance as

well as registration but it also took the direct employment of dock labour out of the hands of port employers. Of course Bevin was able to justify the introduction of the scheme on the basis of the needs of the wartime emergency. He argued that it was necessary if the war effort was not to be hampered by the slow turn round of shipping. Thus, in his introduction to the scheme Bevin wrote:

> The Government has decided that as a wartime measure to secure the quicker turnround of ships in ports, all registered dock workers at the following places: Liverpool (including Birkenhead), Manchester, Preston, Garston, Bamborough, Ellesmere Port, Partington, Widnes, Runcorn and Western Point, shall be employed by the Minister of Transport on a guaranteed weekly basis combined where possible with payment by results. In this way it is hoped to build up a regular mobile labour force to handle rapidly and efficiently the heavy traffic which is passing through these ports.[2]

Further, Bevin publically stated that in his view "transport had become the key to victory and the complete and effective organisation of transport would determine the duration of the war".[3] He suggested that by introducing the west coast scheme he might achieve a 40 percent quicker turnround in shipping. However, it is also clear that Bevin could have justified the scheme, maybe with the details rather different but with a similar overall structure, without reference to the needs of the war. The scheme fitted in with his well established views about how dock labour should be engaged and about how the worst manifestations of the casual system of employment could be overcome.

Originally it had been intended that the scheme should apply to all west coast ports but there was resistance from the Clyde ports and they were left out of the scheme that was introduced in March 1941. Nevertheless, the Government was determined that eventually they should be brought within the scheme and continued to press the issue. In April of the same year a ballot was taken of Glasgow dockers to see if they would accept the scheme: 188 voted for the scheme, but 2,405 against. This vote persuaded the Government to take a more decisive stand: the Minister of Transport issued an ultimatum in which he said that Glasgow dockers either had to accept the scheme or leave the industry. The union organising the dockers decided to ask their members to give the scheme a three months trial, and despite continuing hostility the scheme was finally introduced in the Clyde ports.

The west coast ports were seen to be particularly important for the war effort and therefore initially attention was focused on them. However, it was always intended that similar action should be taken to alter employment practices in all British ports. Bevin announced his intention of doing so almost immediately the Ministry of Transport scheme had been introduced in the west coast ports. He told dockers and their employers that he intended to bring dock work within the scope of the Essential Work Orders which had already been introduced in some industries and asked them to consider agreeing the basis of a registration and maintenance scheme for all dock workers not covered by the Ministry of Transport scheme. A national docks delegate conference of the Transport and General Workers' Union was called for 20 June 1941 and this conference agreed to set up an emergency sub-committee to negotiate on the matter. Similar moves were made by the port employers. Later in 1941 the employers and the trade unions, through the National Joint Council for the Port Transport Industry, agreed a draft scheme and this was put to the Minister. The scheme was introduced in the larger ports in September 1941 and then gradually extended to the smaller ones at a later date.[4] Virtually all dockers in major British ports were covered either by this or the Ministry of Transport scheme by the end of 1943.

The scheme introduced in September 1941 was under the direction of a new body, the National Dock Labour Corporation. The corporation was a limited company and composed of twelve trade union and twelve employer representatives. It delegated many of its powers to its Board of Directors (itself composed of three union and three employer representatives along with an independent chairman and a finance director appointed by the Minister of Labour and National Service). The trade unions were represented on the Board of Directors by two officials from the Transport and General Workers' Union (Deakin and Milford) and one official from the National Amalgamated Stevedores and Dockers (Turner).

The National Dock Labour Corporation was the legal employer of all dock workers in the ports it covered. Existing port employers no longer had the right to hire dockers directly though most were recognised as "approved employers" and effectively sub-contracted labour from the Corporation. As in the west coast ports, dockers were offered maintenance through the provisions of this scheme, though it took a rather different form. Instead of being given guaranteed earnings dockers were offered attendance money if they turned up for work but were not offered employment (5 shillings a half-day). The costs of the scheme were met largely by the "approved employers". They had to make two payments: one was to cover the dockers' normal wages, the other was to contribute to the National Management Pool from which the cost of attendance payments was met (the level of payment into the pool varied from 25 to 10 percent of the wages bill).

Wartime Problems

The wartime schemes for the registration and maintenance of dock labour improved the position of dock workers in many ways. One of the most obvious was the guarantee of regular earnings. However, in order to obtain such guaranteed earnings dockers had to turn up for work regularly, and many of them, partly because they were not used to such restrictions, failed to do so. The irregular work practices of dockers did not simply affect their earnings, though; they also affected the ability of the ports to offer a quick turnround of ships, and an improvement in the efficiency and speed with which cargo was handled was the main official reason for the introduction of both wartime dock labour schemes.

Bevin, as the main architect of the wartime schemes, clearly was eager to improve the position. In part, his reputation was at stake: but so too was the future of the schemes which he so passionately believed to be in the best interests of dock workers. In February 1942 Bevin and the Minister of War Transport invited representatives of employers and unions to meet them in conference at Caxton Hall, London. 300 union and 250 employers' representatives attended and heard Bevin argue that if improvements in port efficiency and speed of turnaround were not made then military control of the ports would be the only alternative.

In the following months a number of attempts were made to improve the position in the ports. The Transport and General Workers' Union told its members that the working rule book was to be withdrawn; in March 1942 the Regional Port Director for the North West announced that an "honour" system would be introduced in the Merseyside ports under which dockers would no longer be required to accept employment when offered, nor would they be subject to the disciplinary provisions of the dock labour scheme, but instead they would be placed on their "honour" to make the scheme work. The first "honour week" began on 1 June and the Regional Director claimed that it had been a success. For example, he said, that during the week only 1.4 percent of workers had refused offers of employment, when under the scheme they should have accepted them, and only 1.75 percent would have incurred disciplinary action had the normal provisions of the scheme applied. As a result of this "success" the experiment was continued for a further period.

Some people, however, took exception to the introduction of the system in particular, and, more generally, to working practices on Merseyside. A letter was published in a local newspaper criticising labour practices later in 1942 and, partly as a result (though the link was strongly denied in the House of Commons), an inquiry was set up into working conditions on the Merseyside docks, and extended later to cover the whole of the North West region. The inquiry, under the chairmanship of Sir John Foster, reported later in 1942, though the report was never published. However, it led to the resignation of the Regional Port Director. It is also worthwhile noting that later, in evidence to the Amman inquiry, it was claimed that in Liverpool in 1942 20 per cent of registered dockers were failing to attend call places as they were required. In the following years, the position on Merseyside improved, although problems continued to arise: for example, in 1943 a dispute arose which led to 35 men being suspended for refusing to work overtime and this led to a stoppage throughout the Merseyside ports.

The labour problems in British ports during the war were by no means confined to Merseyside. Serious disputes arose, for example, in London, Manchester and Bristol and in most ports the dock labour schemes ran into operational problems. Towards the end of 1945 a major unofficial strike took place involving 40,000 dockers and affecting most of Britain's major ports. The strike was over a national wage claim, which the dockers felt was not being pressed strongly enough. In fact, the Transport and General Workers' Union had already made moves which, had they been known, might have satisfied the dockers, but these moves had not been made public. The strike was eventually settled after a secret ballot of union members, but in the meantime troops had been brought in by the Government to unload ships and move essential supplies. The union leaders clearly saw the strike partly as an attack on them and as a comment on their willingness and ability to press the dockers' case. In December 1945 the Acting General Secretary of the Transport and General Workers' Union reported to the Executive Council:

> Arising from the dispute it will, I think, be necessary for the Council to order an inquiry into activities of certain unofficial elements in London, Liverpool and Hull, particularly in relation to the suggestions that have been made against the Docks Officers. The National Secretary, and the Area Group Officers in many cases, are highly incensed in relation to the allegations of no confidence that have been made, and have demanded the protection of the Executive against the sort of insinuations and attempts made to destroy the confidence of the membership in them.[5]

Some of the problems and disputes during the war were to be expected for new demands and patterns of employment were being imposed on dockers. The problems were not such that the supporters of the schemes were not able to maintain that without the schemes the ability of the ports to meet the needs of the war effort would have been seriously reduced. However, one element of the disputes, the attack on the official union leadership was viewed more seriously, and subsequently was to become a major cause for concern.

After the War

Considerable attention had been paid during the War to the basis of employment in the port transport industry after the cessation of hostilities. As early as 1941 the Acting General Secretary of the Transport and General Workers' Union was telling his executive Council that the schemes being introduced during the war could have long-term significance:

> It may well be that the scheme (the east coast scheme) will provide a basis upon which

to build a post war arrangement for the docks which will go far to remove our members from the casual nature of employment against which we have struggled for many years.[6]

A similar point was made by Bevin two years later: "... the guaranteed week must not go with the war". He wanted those men who had done the fighting to come back and feel that while they were away their jobs had been made more secure and worth coming back to.

No one should be tempted to break it (the Dock Labour Scheme) up. It was a wonderful thing for a woman to know when she was bringing up her children what her man was going to bring home and when he was going to bring it home - they never knew that under the casual system that existed before.[7]

More detailed discussions about what would happen after the end of the war began in 1944. The Transport and General Workers' Union began to make moves to consolidate their policy holding a special conference of dock officers and a National Dock Delegate Conference in the early autumn. The union was determined to maintain the kind of scheme introduced during the war: they wanted a national scheme which was jointly controlled and offered guaranteed earnings. However, they were aware that the employers favoured some move away from the wartime schemes, preferring a series of local schemes to one national scheme. Discussions held with the Government suggested to Transport and General Workers' Union Officers that they might get government support for most of their own proposals: nevertheless, the Government argued that a scheme jointly agreed between the workpeople and the employers in the industry would be preferable to an imposed one.

The discussions on a post-war dock labour scheme took place in the National Joint Council for the industry. Although there was initial disagreement between some of the workpeople's representatives (principally because the Scottish Transport and General Workers' Union wanted a separate scheme for Glasgow) eventually they agreed on a common plan. However, the discussions failed to produce agreement between the workpeople and the employers. Two central issues illustrate the dissention between them. First, the workpeople demanded joint control of a national scheme, along the lines of the east coast wartime scheme, while the employers argued for local schemes (within a national framework) controlled by the port authorities. Second, the workpeople wanted a guaranteed weekly wage and attendance payments (a mixture of the provisions of the east and west coast wartime schemes) while the employers only offered a guaranteed monthly wage (later modified to a guaranteed week).

The failure of the two sides of the industry to reach agreement led the Government to introduce the Dock Workers (Regulation of Employment) Act of 1946 which prolonged the life of the wartime schemes while discussions on their future were taking place, and later in 1946 the Government asked Sir John Forster to hold an inquiry into the matter. The report of the Forster inquiry was published in December 1946.[8] On many issues the report backed the views of the workpeople's side of the National Joint Council. For example, Forster argued in favour of a scheme organised by a national joint committee supported by local subsidiary joint committees. Thus, he said:

In my view the decasualisation scheme most likely to prove successful would be one administered by a central body of the character of the National Docks Labour Corporation whose central board should be drawn in equal numbers from the two sides of the port transport industry and to which should be added an independent element consisting of a Chairman and two members appointed by the Minister of Labour.[9]

However, he accepted the employers' arguments over earnings. Thus he suggested that there should be simply a guaranteed weekly wage and he went on to declare that although the guarantee should be "sufficient to meet a workers' minimum needs" it should not be "so high as to constitute a temptation to him to rely upon the guarantee rather than the actual employment".[10]

In March 1947 the Government published a draft order embodying most of the proposals of the Forster report. However, the proposals on guaranteed earnings and attendance money were not dealt with and both sides were given an opportunity to lodge objections to the proposals contained in the draft order. The objections were considered by an inquiry under the chairmanship of J Cameron and led to some changes in the detail of the proposals. For example, some of the objections to the exclusion of certain ports from the draft scheme were upheld: Cameron recommended that Birkenhead and Newcastle should be added to the list of ports covered by the scheme. Similarly some of the objections to certain classes of employment being included under the scheme were upheld: Cameron suggested that timber trade workers normally engaged in saw mills should be excluded. Despite these changes in detail the Cameron inquiry confirmed the basic plan and left the centre of the scheme untouched.

The one main issue on which the Forster inquiry had recommended in favour of the employers, earnings, because it had been left out of the draft order, was not considered by the Cameron inquiry. Further discussion between employers and workpeople's representatives failed to produce an agreement and a separate inquiry was held into this issue under the chairmanship of H J W Hetherington.[11] On the central point this inquiry found in favour of the position put forward by the workpeople's representatives: it recommended a system involving both attendance payments and a guaranteed weekly wage. The recommended level of both payments was a compromise between the suggestions of the workpeople's and the employers' representatives, but this does not detract from the fact that on the central issue the workpeople gained what they had wanted.

The resolution of the disagreement over earnings paved the way for the Minister of Labour to introduce the Dock Workers (Regulation of Employment) Order into Parliament in June 1947. Under the terms of the Order a new National Dock Labour Scheme was introduced with the following provisions:

(i)   The establishment of a national administering board with local boards at the ports.

(ii)   The registration of employers and workers who thereupon are deemed to have accepted the obligations of the scheme.

(iii)   A prohibition of registered employers from engaging dock labour other than registered workers.

(iv)   That registered daily workers, where not employed in pursuance of the scheme by any other employer, are in the employment of the National Board and if they are available for work, they are then in the reserve pool.

(v)   A prohibition on registered workers from engaging for work with a registered employer except as weekly workers or being selected by a registered employer or allocated to him in accordance with the scheme.

(vi)   A corresponding obligation on the employers to accept the daily workers so allocated and on the workers to accept the employment.

(vii)   The control of wages paid by the employers and entitlement of workers in the reserve pool to payment from the National Board (remuneration due from employers in respect of daily workers being paid to the National Board).

(viii)   Disciplinary powers (including provisions for disentitlement of workers to payment for non-compliance with certain provisions of the scheme) and provisions for the termination of employment of daily workers, for appeals by persons aggrieved to appeal tribunals, and for the cost of the operation of the scheme.[12]

Prior to the Second World War a number of the provisions introduced through the 1947 Order had been in operation at certain ports: during the war others were introduced on a wider basis.   However, the 1947 Order nevertheless presented a major extension of past practice because it introduced a range of provisions, (some of which had operated in individual ports) to all major ports in Britain through one national scheme.   Further the provisions, where they had existed prior to the war, had relied on voluntary agreement; now they were to be enforced by law.

The 1947 Order, then, marked a major extension of, if not departure from, previous practice.   Nevertheless, it is important to record that it did not eradicate the casual system of employment from the docks.   The 1947 order controlled and regulated employment but employment remained casual for most dockers.   In this sense the 1947 order clearly built on the early moves to deal with the casual system of employment in the industry for it was based on registration and maintenance rather than decasualisation.

The Attitude of the Transport and General Workers' Union

The officials of the Transport and General Workers' Union, as has been noted many times, played an important role in pressing the case for registration and maintenance before the Second World War.   At the outbreak of war they redoubled their efforts.   A resolution passed by the docks group in the autumn of 1939 complained about the lack of progress on decasualisation, and the General Secretary in his report to the Executive Council backed the resolution, saying that it was completely justified and asked for "authority to take steps at the opportune moment to bring these matters to a head". [3]   Of course, as has been noted, when Bevin became Minister of Labour during the war, he had the ideal opportunity to take measures in the name of the war effort which he had been striving over a period of about thirty years.

The difficulties faced in the early stages of the wartime schemes did not lead the Union to abandon its support for the schemes.   To the contrary, union leaders acted decisively to deal with the problems.   The way in which the Transport and General Workers' Union agreed to withdraw the working rule book in February 1942 was a testimony to the seriousness of their intent: the fact that they were persuaded to do so by Bevin was also "proof of the authority Bevin still commanded in the trade union movement and of his willingness to use it". [14]

At the end of the war the Transport and General Workers' Union officials determined to use all possible avenues of persuasion to ensure that the wartime schemes were not abandoned.   In January 1945, for example, the National Docks Group Committee decided that, the policy should be "to concentrate all our efforts to secure permanent decasualisation, and to adjourn consideration of an application for an increase in wages and alteration in conditions". [15]

In large part the policy of the Transport and General Workers' Union was sustained by Bevin's efforts.   Bevin's commitment to registration and maintenance was well known by the time he became Minister of Labour: as his biographer, Bullock, said, it was "the cause which had first won him a reputation as a trade union leader".[16] However, it would be wrong to suggest that Bevin was the only supporter of registration and maintenance during this period. A number of other leading union officials were firmly committed to the same policy. For example, when the West Coast scheme was accepted by the Merseyside dockers, the national docks officer, Donovan, said that he "viewed the scheme as a milestone in the life of the docker".[17] Later the same year, Harry Edwards, addressing the National Conference of the Transport and General Workers' Union as its chairman, said that to him as a docker, it had been a source of great satisfaction to live to see the introduction of principles designed to abolish casual employment in dockland.[18] Deakin, Bevin's successor (first acting and then in his own right) as General Secretary of the Transport and General workers' Union, did not have the same direct experience on the docks as Bevin. Nevertheless, he developed a keen interest in the affairs of dockers. Partly he was directly influenced in this area, as in so many others, by Bevin's ideas, but also partly he was reacting "to the deplorable conditions of employment on the docks".[19]

The attitude, certainly of the leadership of the Transport and General Workers' Union, towards efforts to deal with the problems of casual employment in the docks over this period has been well summarised by Vic Allen. He argues that, in "the matter of decasualisation of dock labour the union had developed its own momentum".[20] The moves to change the system of employment on the docks had been pressed for so many years, and with such fervour, in particular by Bevin, that few officers ever even seriously considered that the policy might not be the right one to pursue.

As in earlier periods, one of the attractions of the moves made to regularise employment on the docks, was that it might help to strengthen the union's position both in respect of non-members and other unions. However, while this motive should not be discounted, neither should it be seen as the only one. The earlier references indicate how many leaders believed that regularisation of employment would be of major benefit to the dockers themselves, and, as Allen argued, by the end of the Second World War, the objectives of decasualisation were rarely rehearsed. It is interesting to note in this context, that, in some instances, the regularisation of employment seemed to be threatening, not aiding, union membership. This concern was reported to the National Executive of the union, with the particular example of Merseyside being given, during the war.

> The National Secretary reported union difficulties that had been experienced in relation to the payment of Union contributions on Merseyside following the introduction of the North Western scheme, due to a tendency on the part of certain of the men to regard the union as being no longer necessary to protect their interests.[21]

Such problems did not lead the Union to question its support for the particular schemes, or the moves to regularise employment in general: rather they were perceived as another of the obstacles that had to be overcome in pursuit of its primary goal.

The Attitude of Union Members

The moves to alleviate the effects of the casual system of employment on the docks, made by the Transport and General Workers' Union, it has been argued, were a continuation of similar moves before the war. The reaction of union members in some ports to the wartime schemes also echoed earlier attitudes. One of the ports where pre-war opposition was most vocal was the scene of conflict during the War. The Glasgow dockers made it clear, when attempts were made to include them in the west coast scheme, that their opposition to registration was as strong as ever. Thus, a report in The Times noted:

> Glasgow dockers, unwilling to accept the provisions of the docks reorganisation scheme, are asking that Mr Ernest Bevin, Minister of Labour, should go to Clydeside and discuss the details with them. It is stated that it is the principle of registration to which they mainly object. Clydeside dockers claim that the casual system is so efficient in wartime that where normally a ship would require six days turnaround, now it is able to depart in four.[22]

This argument, that their methods of operating were as efficient and had the same beneficial effects as registration, was exactly the same as that used in the 1920s and 1930s. The later agreement to work the scheme by Glasgow dockers was not an indication that they had accepted the wisdom of the transport Union's official position (the union they had left) on such matters: it was simply a reflection of the ability of the Government, in wartime conditions, to coerce them into working the scheme.

The wartime schemes were opposed more fiercely at Glasgow than elsewhere, but a reluctance and apprehension was evident at many other ports. This was explicitly recognised by national officers of the Transport and General Workers' Union. In 1942, Donovan, then National Docks Group Secretary, in a report to the National Executive Council of the Transport and General Workers' Union said:

> Revolutionary changes have taken place in the methods of employing port labour. In January 1941 the Minister of Labour and National Service and the Minister of War Transport indicated that they proposed to bring the whole of the port transport workers in the Clyde and Merseyside areas into the Employment of the Ministry of War Transport at a guaranteed wage equal to eleven half-days, i.e. 4.2s.6d. per week. In return the men would be under obligation to report twice a day, and to be available for any suitable employment on offer, including transfer from port to port. These schemes created acute problems inasmuch as men were suddenly called upon to change habits of a lifetime. At first some suspicion and difficulty was experienced in getting the members to appreciate that these guaranteed payments were intended to give them economic security in order that they should be available for this essential work.[23]

Many dockers, particularly those left in the industry during the war were older and had a lifetime's experience on the docks. They were particularly loathe to give up the freedom and the working practices which had been developed to give them greater control over the work process and preserve jobs. While during the war there was plenty of work and a shortage of labour, the position could change, and most could remember the difficulties of the 1930's. Moreover, the benefits they were being offered in return for giving up these practices were not as real as they seemed at first sight. Although average earnings rose (in the last quarter of 1942 dockers' average weekly earnings were 12.2 per cent higher than the national average for adult males, whereas by 1944, they were 33.3 per cent higher), the guaranteed payments meant little while work was readily available and while high earnings could be obtained from a shortened working week. They also meant little to the best organised and high status groups on the docks, like the stevedores. It threatened to break up the privileged position they had gained, destroying their gangs and making them share work with others, offering them in return a level of guaranteed earnings that bore little relationship to what the most favoured in the industry could be expected to achieve.

Undoubtedly, Donovan was right in arguing that the changes demanded in working habits and attitudes were one of the main reasons why dockers in many ports felt uneasy about the introduction of the wartime schemes. However, he also recognised another reason for this unease, and one which had just as important long-term implications. Many dockers were worried about the secondment of their union officials to the Ministry of War Transport, as they were later about the Union's agreement to abandon established work practices. Both items indicated the close identification of the Transport and General Workers' Union with the wartime schemes, an identification that was continued in the 1947 scheme.

The disputes between dockers and scheme officials caused serious problems at many ports throughout the war. In a number of cases the disputes were sufficiently serious to need official inquiries. Earlier the Forster inquiry at Merseyside was mentioned; the Doughty inquiry[24] into the stoppage at Grimsby is another example. The Transport and General Workers' Unions's officers argued that the disputes were "due more to personal factors rather than to there being anything wrong with the structure of the schemes":[25] however, to attempt to explain the disputes, simply on the basis of personal factors, would be an oversimplification. Some of the other factors, recognised earlier by Transport and General Workers' Union officials themselves, were also important.

Towards the end of the War a major stoppage occurred in the port of London which indicated the range of issues concerning the operation of the schemes over which problems were occurring, not simply during their introduction and the early stages of their operation, when one might have expected "teething" problems to have arisen, but after the schemes had been in existence for a number of years. The stoppage began in the Royal group of docks on 2 March 1945 over a decision to change the location of a call-on stand. Although arrangements were made to restore the call-stand to its original position, pending an investigation, and so deal with the initial dispute, the stoppage continued and eventually covered the whole of the port of London. The list of grievances was extended to cover a series of complaints about the operation of the Dock Labour Scheme in general and the disciplinary position in particular. At one point the stoppage extended to Tilbury. Eventually the Union leaders were able to persuade the dockers to suspend their action but only "on the understanding that there would be a full inquiry into the administration of the Dock Labour Scheme in the port of London".[26]

Later in 1945 strikes occurred in a number of other ports over the operation of the schemes: for example, stoppages occurred at Newport in March, and at Leith, Aberdeen and Hull in June. Earlier the strike over the national wage claim, which also took place in 1945, was reported.

Of course such strikes, and others that followed, were not directed to obtaining the abolition of the dock labour schemes. Nevertheless, some were an indication of dissatisfaction with the way that the schemes were operating and the dissatisfaction sprung not simply from detailed maladministration but from more fundamental aspects of their provision, such as their disciplinary machinery and regulations. The inquiry into the strike in London in March 1945,[27] for example, argued that the strike had its origins in the dockers' feeling of "resentment against the harsh exercise of discipline"[28] at the port, while Allen argued that the "strike indicated that the war-time schemes in certain instances might have been operating at the margin of the men's tolerance; that the cost of decasualisation to dockers in terms of liberty of action could outweigh the social and economic advantages".[29]

The issue might be expressed as one of control. The new schemes threatened to take control away from the docker; control over issues like who could work on the docks, where a docker had to work and the allocation of work. This latter issue could be particularly contentious. The managers of dock labour boards frequently gained powers to direct registered workers to the employers that needed them. They could do so ignoring established lines of demarcation and specialism. The controls over the docker were mediated by the involvement of the union. For many dockers, though, this did not solve the problem; it merely led them to question which side the union leader was really on.

Notes

1. This problem was not unique to the docks, but extended to most "essential" industries. For example, see experience in the coal mining industry.
2. Ministry of Labour, *Dock Labour in Merseyside, Manchester and Preston areas: Explanatory Memorandum,* HMSO, London, 1941, p1.
3. Times, 28 February 1941, p4.
4. At the end of 1942 the scheme covered 32,000 workers: by the end of 1943 the total had risen to almost 39,000 and by June 1944 to almost 43,000.
5. Acting General Secretary's Report to the Transport and General Workers' Union's General Executive Council, 6 December 1945, p285.
6. Acting General Secretary's Report to the Transport and General Workers' Union's General Executive Council, 8 September 1941, p271.
7. Times, 6 September 1943, p2.
8. Ministry of Labour and National Service, *Report of Inquiry held under Paragraph 1(4) of the Schedule to the Dock Workers (Regulation of Employment) Act 1946,* HMSO, London 1946.
9. Quoted in Times, 9 December 1946, p2.
10. *Ibid.*
11. See, Ministry of Labour and National Service, *Report of a Committee of Inquiry into the Amount and Basis of Calculation of the Guaranteed Wage to be made to Dock Workers under the Dock Workers* (Regulation of Employment) Scheme, 1947, HMSO, London, 1947.
12. Dock Workers (Regulation of Employment) Order, 1947. Taken from Halsbury's Statutory Instruments.
13. General Secretary's Report to the General Executive Council 14 August, 1939, p356.
14. A Bullock, *The Life and Times of Ernest Bevin,* Vol I, Heinemann, London, 1960, p209.
15. Annual Report and Trade Group Review, Transport and General Workers' Union, 1945-6, p39.
16. A Bullock, *Op Cit,* p58.
17. Times, 1 March 1941, p2.
18. Times, 19 August 1941, p2.
19. V Allen, *Trade Union Leadership,* Longman, London, 1957, p174.
20. *Ibid,* p174.
21. Transport and General Workers' Union, General Executive Council Minutes, 3 March 1943, min.174.
22. Times, 7 March 1941, p9.
23. Annual Report, Transport and General Workers' Union, 1941-2, pp63-4.
24. Referred to in the Annual Report and Trade Group Review of the Transport and General Workers' Union, 1941-2.
25. Annual Report, Transport and General Workers' Union, 1943-4, p58.
26. General Executive Council Minutes, 5 March 1945, minute 145, p33.
27. Report of Committee of Inquiry into the London Dock Dispute, March 1945, HMSO, London, 1945.
28. *Ibid,* p4. Also quoted by V Allen, *Op Cit,* at p186.

5 Post war years

1947 Dock Labour Scheme and its Problems

The 1947 Dock Labour Scheme was seen by many trade union leaders and social reformers as the culmination of years of effort to improve the position of dock workers. Some recognised its limitations: it did not eliminate the casual system of employment but simply regulated it and alleviated some of its worst effects. Nevertheless, few would have predicted the problems (certainly their extent and the depth of feeling they brought forth) that arose during the early years of the operation of the scheme.

Many of the problems can be illustrated by reference to a number of strikes that occurred in the late 1940s and early 1950s. Throughout the late 1940s and early 1950s the port transport industry experienced a significant increase in strike activity. For example, in the period 1947 to 1955, on average 3,134 working days were lost through strikes each year for every 1,000 insured workers in the industry, compared to 285 working days per 1,000 insured workers in the period 1930 to 1938. The increase was not simply a reflection of national trends: by 1947 to 1955 dock workers were the most strike prone group of workers in Britain (if measured by the number of working days lost through strikes) with, for example, about four times as many days lost through strikes (per 1,000 workers) as coal miners. However, while the strikes provide a convenient and vivid way of illustrating the problems facing the new Dock LabourScheme, they are only an illustration, and the problems themselves were felt far more extensively than the strikes. Further, there are some problems which may have been background factors behind strikes but, at least, were not the reasons cited as the cause of the strike.

Four main problems will be highlighted in the discussion that follows: the joint control of the scheme, discipline (which is centrally related to the issue of joint control), the obligations of the scheme, and the size of the register. The second and the third problems can be illustrated by reference to major strikes and official inquiries: the first and fourth problems surfaced in less dramatic fashion, but were no less important.

Joint Control

The principle of joint control was central to the 1947 Dock Labour Scheme. It had been an issue of debate between the unions and employers prior to the scheme being set up, but had been recommended by the Forster inquiry[1]. The inquiry had supported joint control because of the previous experience in the industry (the interwar registration schemes were jointly controlled by employers and unions) and because the unions had made it clear that they would only cooperate with a scheme that was jointly controlled, while everyone, including the employers, recognised that union cooperation was essential for the success of any scheme.

Joint control was important at both the national and local levels. The National Dock Labour Board was composed of an equal number of trade union employer representatives, plus an independent element. The local dock labour boards, which supervised most of the detailed operation of the scheme, also had equal representation from trade unions and employers, but did not have an independent element. Joint control, in practice, meant that decisions over the size of the register and discipline were decided jointly by the two sides and it meant that the administration of the scheme, including the payment of wages, was jointly controlled: however, matters like the level of wages were not dealt with on this basis but remained an issue for negotiation between the two sides.

The employers never accepted the joint control of the scheme. They continued to press their opposition despite the recommendations of the Forster inquiry and their resolve to do so was strengthened by the industrial relations problems that faced the industry during the late 1940s and early 1950s. Reference has already been made to the increase in strike activity during this period and later some of the major strikes will be looked at in more detail. However, one of the major causes of concern was not simply the extent of industrial conflict, but also its nature. Most of the strikes that occurred were unofficial and opposed by the main trade unions: many were run by unofficial committees and after a strike in 1948 the committee running that strike continued to operate under the name of the Port Workers' Committee. The development of what is sometimes referred to as an "unofficial movement" on the docks in the late 1940s and early 1950s, in some ways a permanent opposition and alternative to the official trade unions, with its own semi-formal structure, was a crucial development and an indication to the port employers of a fundamental problem facing the industry.

In their evidence to the committee of inquiry appointed in 1955 under the chairmanship of Mr Justice Devlin, the employers argued that joint control had been the source of most of the industry's problems:

> It had been hoped that the scheme (the 1947 scheme) would make the docks industry happier than the average, but it has not been so. The employers attribute this result to the nature of the scheme - not to any particular provision of it but to its main concept, namely, the principle of dual control. The position of trade union leaders on the Board, their taking part in the function of management, has, the employers believe, weakened their authority with the men and led them into a conflict of duty, dividing their loyalty between the Board and the men they lead. This is, in the employers' view, the fundamental source of unrest in the industry. As the Scheme stands, the employers say, they can do nothing to cure it, because they cannot get into direct relationship with their own workpeople.[2]

In essence, then, the argument was that joint control meant that the unions, particularly the main union, the Transport and General Workers' Union had become part of the management of the industry, and as a result had lost the confidence of its own members. To support this argument the employers quoted from a number of Bulletins of the unofficial movements and Broadsheets of the National Amalgamated Stevedores and Dockers union (which, by this time, was not represented on the National Dock Labour Board).

1   "Port Workers' News" Special Supplement, February, 1954

But the policy and actions of the present leadership of the Transport and General Workers' Union often appears to members as giving way to employers rather than fighting determinedly for the wishes of the members. Indeed, the leadership has to a considerable degree lost the respect and confidence of large sections of the membership.

2   NASD Broadsheets:

(a) No 16 (16 April 1955)

Then came the war, and the MOWT's dock scheme. The attitude of the Transport and General Workers' Union was to ensure that the scheme worked, even if this meant that it worked against the men.

(b)No 20 (May 1955)

For years now the employers in this country have disciplined the workers through the "constitutionalists and right wing leaders of the trade unions movement".

3   NASD Bulletin

No 6 (3 June 1955)

In practice the Transport and General Workers' Union has become an instrument through which the employers carry out their policy.[3]

The case of the National Amalgamated Stevedores and Dockers union, whose Bulletin is referred to above, is an interesting one. When the National Dock Labour Board was set up they took one of the seats on it, but in 1949 their representative on the Board led a strike against one of its decisions and subsequently the union was excluded from membership. The position of the Stevedores union is complicated and will be referred to again later, but for the moment it is worthwhile recalling that this incident illustrates one of the pressures of joint control: collective responsibility for joint decisions (even if made on a majority vote) versus the need to pursue the policies demanded by union members.

The Transport and General Workers' Union disputed the employers' reading of the situation. They argued that there need not be any conflict between collective responsibility and the freedom of unions to pursue their own policy because union members of the National (and local) Dock Labour Board were nominees, not representatives. Thus, the union need not accept the decision of the Board even if their nominee had agreed to it.

The 1956 Devlin inquiry broadly accepted the arguments of the union and rejected those of the employers. It suggested the retention of the principle of joint control and argued that union members opposedcooperation with employers, not participation in the Scheme. It concluded that the problems of the industry were not directly linked to the character of the Dock Labour Scheme. It said that after "eight years, working there (was) much to be put to the credit of the scheme. A large administrative machinery (was) working smoothly and efficiently"[4].

Discipline

One of the most important areas of joint control under the 1947 Scheme was that of discipline. Under the terms of the scheme employers had no power to discipline workers directly: if they wanted disciplinary action to be taken against an employee then they had to report them to the local manager of the Dock Labour Board who would normally deal with the matter. Provisions also existed for an appeal by the worker against a local managers decision and such an appeal was heard by a local joint committee (composed of equal numbers of employers and employees representatives). The disciplinary provisions were modified somewhat in 1953 after a court case, Barnard v National Dock Labour Board[5], in which it was held that the widespread practice of delegating disciplinary powers to the local manager (rather than the local boards dealing directly with the matter themselves) was ultra vires. Subsequently local boards dealt directly with disciplinary cases. The local boards, either directly or indirectly, had a variety of penalties at their disposal when dealing with disciplinary issues: these ranged from disentitlement to the payments normally made under the scheme, to suspension and ultimately dismissal.

The first major challenge to the exercise of discipline under the scheme came with what became known as the zinc-oxide strike. The strike began in London on 12 June 1948 as a protest against the disciplinary action taken against eleven men who had refused to unload a cargo of zinc-oxide. The men claimed that the cargo was dirty and that they should be paid extra for unloading it. Their claim was turned down and when, as a result, they refused to unload the cargo, they were suspended for seven days and entitlement to attendance money and the guaranteed fallback wage was withdrawn for thirteen weeks. The men appealed against the penalties and after a local appeal tribunal failed to agree, an independent committee appointed by the Minister of Labour decided that the suspensions should be upheld but that the withdrawal of attendance and fallback payments should be reduced from the initial period of thirteen to two weeks.

Dock workers in London refused to accept the penalties and went on strike. The strike spread throughout the port and eventually to Merseyside. It was only settled after the government threatened to call a "state of emergency" and when they agreed to return to work (some two weeks after the strike had begun) the dockers made it clear that they were doing so because of the pressure and threats against them rather than because the bone of contention had been settled[6].

The following year a series of strikes occurred in a number of British ports which illustrate another aspect of the way discipline was handled under the 1947 Dock Labour Scheme. The background to the strikes was a dispute between two Canadian seamen's unions, the Seafarers' International Union and the Canadian Seamens' Union. The latter union,which was said to be "Communist dominated", had called a strike over wages and recognition and had asked for support from British dockers.

The first in the series of strikes occurred in May 1949 at Avonmouth when dockers, acting in sympathy with the Canadian Seamens' Union, refused to unload a Canadian ship, the SS Montreal City. Later, the strike spread to Merseyside and it was not until 13 June and 15 June that the strikers returned to work on Merseyside and at the ristol ports respectively.

The return to work at Merseyside and the Bristol ports, however, was not the end of the matter, for later in June dockers in London refused to unload two Canadian ships. The Port of London Authority (one of the main employers) stated that it would not employ men on any work until the two Canadian ships had been unloaded. This particular dispute was quickly settled when the owners of the ships and the Canadian Seamens' Union reached an agreement.

The third and final of the series of strikes started at the end of June. The strikes began because the Canadian union reimposed the blacking of the two ships after a further dispute with their owners. The London dockers refused to unload the ships and eventually 7,000 stopped work.

The most important event of the strike, from the point of view of the disciplinary action and penalties, however, occurred early in July. The refusal of London dockers to return to work, despite appeals to them to do so by the General Secretary of the two main dockers unions in London, led the Government to declare a "state of emergency" and the National Dock Labour Board to threaten that if the strike continued then the Dock Labour Scheme might be withdrawn. The significance of this threat was that the withdrawal of the Dock Labour Scheme was being seen as a disciplinary penalty for the failure of a workforce, rather than just individuals, to accept the obligations of the scheme. Six years later the report of the Devlin Committee of Inquiry argued that such threats should not be made: the withdrawal of the scheme was not a penalty that could or should be used to deal with what it termed "mass discipline". Thus, the report said:

> It is no doubt exasperating to those who have to administer the Scheme to be confronted with mass indiscipline, but it is in our view quite unrealistic to talk of its being jeopardised or suspended as a penalty for disobedience. The fact is that if the Scheme expired, the first and most urgent task for all concerned would be to devise another one with all the essential features of the original.[7]

In fact, the threat to withdraw the scheme was repudiated by the Government, and Lord Annan, who was both Government Chief Whip in the House of Lords and Chairman of the National Dock Labour Board, resigned from the Government as a result. The strike finished soon afterwards, though the series of strikes had led in total to the loss of more than 400,000 working days.

The zinc-oxide and the Canadian Seamens' strikes differed in a number of ways. Crucially the former involved discipline and the latter mass indiscipline. However, they had an important common feature: they illustrated the way in which decisions over disciplinary matters, taken by a body composed of equal numbers of employers and employees representatives, could be a major cause of dispute. In both instances, the anger of the dockers was directed as much against the unions as against the employers. The dockers ignored the appeals of union leaders (in the case of the Canadian seamen's strikes, the appeals of the National Amalgamated Stevedores and Dockers union, as well as those of the Transport and General Workers' Union) and publicly attacked the union leadership.

The dilemma facing the union leadership probably was best illustrated by the zinc oxide strike. The General Secretary of the Transport and General Workers' Union told the strikers that he had some doubts about the way disciplinary penalties could be used under the scheme: in particular he argued that some of the maximum penalties that could be imposed were too high. He went further, and said that after the strike the operation of the disciplinary provisions of the scheme would be investigated. In making these comments he was echoing fears expressed by the union before the scheme had been introduced. However, despite these reservations and promises, Deakin and other union officials argued that the men had to adhere to the existing provisions of the scheme: only later could they be changed. Deakin recognised that in accepting the 1947 scheme the union accepted an obligation to work within the existing terms of the scheme, at least until they could be changed. He was not willing to jeopardise the scheme or the union's central role within it and he was not willing to allow the union to withdraw from its disciplinary machinery or for its responsibilities to be questioned.

The distance between the union hierarchies and the rank and file dockers over such matters undoubtedly was one of the reasons for the success of the unofficial movements during this period. The unofficial leaders organised the strikes and maintained control throughout. The decisions to return to work were taken by meetings organised by the unofficial movements, not by the trade union leaders.

The problems resulting from the operation of the disciplinary machinery and the growth in importance of the unofficial movements were the main reasons for the appointment of the Leggett committee. In its terms of reference, the committee was asked to investigate the problems on the docks in "view of the stoppages that have taken place in the London docks"[8]: the committee reported in 1951.

The committee did not produce an "explanation" for the strikes as such: however, they pointed to a number of contributory factors, including the question of discipline. In the committee's report it was argued that dock workers firmly accepted the Dock Labour Scheme, "in the sense that they (had) no desire to return to prewar conditions and would be opposed to any change which would take them back to these conditions"[9]. However, it was recognised that despite this, a number of issues were "causing a certain amount of dissatisfaction"[10]. One of the issues causing dissatisfaction was discipline. According to the report it was not simply the disciplinary penalties that were causing dissatisfaction but also the machinery for handling questions of discipline: in particular, the participation of union officials in such machinery.

> We have no doubt that the participation of Union officials who are members of the Board in the exercise of the Board's disciplinary powers, and particularly the power of dismissal, has had the effect of damaging the standing of these officials with their Union membership.[11]

The Leggett report argued that the damage caused to the standing of union officials in this way, on top of a number of internal weaknesses within the main union, the Transport and General Workers' Union (for example, the relatively low ratio of union officers to members, and the poor communications between leaders and dockers) was one of the most important explanations for the growth of the unofficial movement.

The Leggett report also drew attention to the problems of using the disciplinary machinery to deal with industrial disputes.

> When attempts have been made to involve disciplinary action against a number of men who are collectively in breach of the Scheme, there has sometimes been confusion and resentment among the men because it has appeared to them that an industrial dispute which except for the Scheme, would have been a clear cut issue between the employers and themselves, is now being turned immediately into a disciplinary issue and statutory penalties are taking the place of traditional methods of settling the dispute. This is regarded by many of the men as external interference in the collective relationships between employers and workers and, rightly or wrongly, gives rise to a feeling of resentment of which unofficial leaders have made much use.[12]

The report also noted the practical difficulties involved in trying to invoke disciplinary penalties in such cases.

Despite these and other comments, the Leggett report did not recommend any major changes to the operation of the Dock Labour Scheme. In particular, it did not recommend a fundamental revision (although it did suggest minor revisions) of the disciplinary procedure and machinery, nor did it recommend any general change to the principal of joint control.

Overtime

One of the requirements of the Dock Labour Scheme was that a registered dock worker had to "work for such periods as (were) reasonable in this particular case"[13]. The precise meaning of this requirement was a matter of dispute between the two sides of the industry: the employers maintained that as a last resort there was an obligation on a docker to work overtime if it was necessary in a particular situation whereas the unions maintained that in principle overtime was voluntary. In the early years of the scheme's operation, these differing interpretations of the position resulted in major conflict.

However, in one of the most celebrated cases involving a dispute concerning overtime, the conflict arose not because unions and management held different interpretations about the meaning of the overtime obligation, but because unions and management tried to resolve their differences and change existing practice against the wishes of rank and file dockers. The conflict being referred to occurred in the port of Manchester. After the Second World War, a rule was accepted in the port that employers could only demand overtime of an employee if they had declared the ship to be one on which overtime would be worked at the time it had entered the port. In other words, a distinction was being drawn between "overtime" and "non-overtime ships" and an employer could not switch between the categories to allow overtime to be worked on just one night. In April 1951, the local joint council at the port agreed to change this rule so that, in normal circumstances, dockers would simply have to work overtime "as required". This change was agreed despite the earlier opposition expressed by the local branch of the Transport and General Workers' Union[14]. A strike occurred in the port of Manchester following the refusal of two men to work overtime from 5.00 pm to 7.00 pm on the "Princess Maria Pia" on 23 April and their subsequent suspension for three days. The strike lasted from 25 April until 7 June. It was organised, not by the official trade union representing dockers in the port, the Transport and General Workers' Union, who argued that it could do nothing to defend the disciplined workers because they would not appeal against the suspension, but by the Port Workers' Committee, a body which had been established during the 1951 pay strikes. The conclusion of the strike did not result from a resolution of the issue ostensibly causing the conflict, but according to Simey[15] because of "exhaustion".

Throughout the strike there was evidence of considerable hostility between the Transport and General Workers' Union and the rank and file docker. Part of the reason was that there seemed to have been a belief amongst dock workers that their employer was the Dock Labour Board, on which the union was represented, rather than the Manchester Ship Canal Company. When questioned by a research team from Liverpool University[16] only 50 per cent of dockers said that their employer was the Manchester Ship Canal Company, the balance saying that it was the Dock Labour Board or that they didn't know. Further questioning revealed that 34 per cent of the group who believed that they were employed by the Manchester Ship Canal Company were favourably disposed towards it, but the proportion so disposed rose to 76 per cent for those who believed the Dock Labour Board to be their employer. Of course, another reason for the hostility of dock workers towards the union was the fact that the union had agreed to change the rules on overtime against the wishes of many of their members. An official report[17] on the strike also blamed it, in part, on the wish of the unofficial leaders to take advantage of any opportunity to exploit dissatisfaction, an argument which was a reflection of a theme common in many official reports at that time.

Conflict concerning overtime came to public attention again three years later in the port of London. At the beginning of 1954 a number of members of the National Amalgamated Stevedores and Dockers union were disciplined for refusing to work overtime. This led the union to impose an overtime ban in the port and on 1 October, a mass meeting decided to call for a strike three days later. Another of the unions organising in the port, the Watermen,

Lightmen, Tugmen and Bargemens' union also decided to take strike action on 17 October. A Court of Inquiry was appointed to inquire into the dispute and made its final report in November[18].

The reports of the Court of Inquiry made it clear that one of the reasons for the dispute had been the different interpretations held by the employers, and the National Amalgamated Stevedores and Dockers union, of the obligations under the Dock Labour Scheme to work overtime. However, they also made it clear that another reason for the dispute was the longstanding antagonism between the Stevedores union and the Transport and General Workers' Union, and between the latter union and the unofficial Portworkers Committee. The proposals of the inquiry were that the obligations in the Scheme should be modified to ease the assumption of compulsion.

Control of the Register

The size and the composition of the register had been a contentious issue from the time of the first registration scheme. There were a variety of pressures at work. The employers wanted a register large enough to allow them to obtain labour as and when required, or, if this was not possible, then they wanted to be able to supplement the register during periods of labour shortage. At the same time they were concerned that the register should not be too large, especially if they had to pay maintenance to men on the register but unable to find work. The union, for their part, wanted a register that was of a size so that men could obtain work, but they were under pressure not to allow members to be excluded from it.

In the early years of the Dock Labour Scheme the size and composition of the register caused conflict on a number of occasions. Part of the difficulty was that changes in economic conditions significantly altered the amount of traffic using the ports and therefore altered the demand for labour. A shortage of labour in one year became a surplus the next, only to revert to a shortage again very shortly afterwards. This can be exemplified by referring to the quotations below. They are taken from national newspaper reports over a four year period, 1952-1956. They illustrate the swift changes in the demand for labour and the pressures that were felt as a result.

October 1952

> The levy imposed on the employers of dock labour to meet the cost of the decasualisation scheme will be increased from 16 to $22^1/2$ per cent from Saturday.

> The increase is the result of a decline in trade which has increasingly affected the amount of work on the docks during the past year. At present about one-fifth of the 79,000 dock workers in British ports are idle on an average each day, and the cost of paying attendance money or making-up weekly earnings to the minimum of £4 8s has been rising steadily.

> Between 1950 and November 1951, the number of dockers on the register was allowed to increase to meet demands from the ports from 75,580 to 82,500. Since then it has gone down by nearly 4,000, mainly as the result of young men leaving the industry to secure more regular work.

> The National Dock Labour Board has power to reduce the register, but there is no immediate intention to do so, because all the ports are hoping that business will improve. It is obvious, however, that such a measure will have to be considered if

trade does not improve soon. Possibly an attempt will be made to obtain an authoritative Government forecast of the future level of trade.'[19]

November 1952

The National Dock Labour Board is considering what to do about unemployment on the docks. For many months the reserve of dock labour has been excessive in almost all ports ... The average daily surplus from April to September this year was 12,201 compared to 4,635 in the corresponding period last year. In every week in October the average was more than 15,000 and in one week it exceeded 18,000 ... Action in the present case has been too long delayed. It is now recognised that something should be done to relieve the position. Apart from the burden on commerce of excessive charges, and the waste of manpower, it is not desirable that dockers should have to depend week after week on a fallback wage of £4 8s. It was never intended that it should be used in this way, but rather as something to help them over a temporary thin period. The attitude of the men who are threatening to resist any reduction in the register is short-sighted in the extreme. To maintain a register that is too large must result in reducing the average standard of living of the dockers, and may revive the old ignominious scramble for work.

At the same time frequent changes in the size of the register would tend to develop that sense of insecurity which the dock labour scheme was primarily intended to end.[20]

July 1953

The report of the National Dock Labour Board for 1952 records that ... of the gross total of 6,422 men lost from the main register, more than 3,700 left the industry of their own accord. The report says that many of those who resigned were men in the middle and lower age groups who the industry can ill afford to lose. This tendency will almost certainly be accentuated by the "temporary release scheme".

The need to establish an efficient and balanced labour force is emphasised, the board regarding as an urgent necessity "a labour policy agreed with the national joint council which will enable men on the main register to be offered a reasonable measure of security over a long period".[21]

April 1954

An emergency meeting of the Dock Labour Board at Liverpool has been called to consider a shortage of dockers at the port which is delaying perishable cargoes for the Easter trade. Nearly 100 ships are in the port and about a dozen were discharging at half speed today because of lack of men after reductions of the port register last year when there was a surplus of workers.[22]

November 1954

New dockers are being recruited to handle one of the greatest influxes of pre-Christmas cargoes on Merseyside. More than 2,000 new workers are needed for a temporary register to cope with the rush ... Some of the men may have an opportunity of joining the 17,500 on the port's permanent register.[23]

The Transport and General Workers' Union, who represent the majority of the dockers, have taken the initiative in presenting the demands partly because of pressure from their members since the recent decline in port activity. Under the scheme, men who "prove attendance" by reporting for work twice a day are guaranteed "attendance money" if there is no work to which they can be sent ... During most of the summer there has been a surplus of labour ... Since the holiday period ended the number surplus to requirements has been 12 or 13 per cent of the total labour force. Last week more than 10,000 men received the guaranteed rate ... The men's unions attribute the slackening of work to the effect of the credit squeeze on imports, the fall in exports to Australia and New Zealand since restrictions were introduced on imports there, and the dislocation of shipping movements by the Suez Canal dispute.'[24]

November 1956

Guaranteed weekly wages for dock workers are to be increased by 16s 6d ... The unions had claimed an increase because of the hardship which, they said, was now being experienced by dock workers through a decline in port traffic. Between 6,000 and 7,000 men are surplus to requirements.

The decline in traffic is the result of import cuts in Australia and New Zealand, the Suez Canal dispute, and the effect of the credit squeeze. The London Dock Labour Board have suspended recruitment so that their register of dock workers is reduced by normal wastage.'[25]

A number of attempts were made to deal with such problems but few were successful or without controversy. In 1952, for example, the National Dock Labour Board introduced what it termed a "dormant register". This meant that a docker could elect to be placed on the dormant register, and if he did so, he would be allowed to obtain work outside the industry. However, it was a requirement of remaining on the register that he had to return to work on the docks within six weeks of being given notice that he was required to do so.

This attempt to temporarily reduce the size of the active register was opposed by both the National Amalgamated Stevedores and Dockers Union and the unofficial movement who saw it as an attempt by the employers to evade their requirements under the Dock Labour Scheme. Some of the strength of their opposition was deflected by the voluntary nature of the scheme, but not all. In particular, they argued for more freedom to be given to individual dockers to decide when they wanted to return to the docks, rather than for them to be constrained in this matter by the partisans of the scheme. Although the Transport and General Workers' Union took a different position the dormant register was not particularly successful, and anyway, as has been noted, was soon overtaken by events which meant that there was a shortage rather than a surplus of labour on the docks.

An earlier attempt to deal with the composition, rather than just the size of the register, had similarly met with opposition and also achieved relatively little. In November 1948 the National Dock Labour Board had issued an instruction to local boards stating that they should remove from the registers men who "by reason of failing health or other permanent physical incapacity" were "unable to meet the minimum requirements of the dock labour scheme" or who were "not carrying out their obligations under the scheme to the full"[26]. In the port of London, it was decided, by the local dock labour board, to seek the removal of 32 men from the register. Of those, three were over 80, 20 were over 70, and it was decided that the other nine were unfit for work. The final decision had been taken by the board as a whole, and therefore endorsed by representatives of the main trade unions, including both the Transport and General Workers' Union and the National Amalgamated Stevedores and Dockers union.

Nevertheless, the Stevedores called a strike over the issue, claiming that the men were being removed from the register because of redundancy rather than ineffectiveness. The strike started on 11 April 1949 and at one point involved men from the Transport and General Workers' Union, as well as from the Stevedores union, despite the fact that the former union campaigned against it. The strikers agreed to return to work on 16 April, as the result of an assurance that negotiations over a retirement allowance for dockers would be speeded up. However, the relatively short duration of the strike should not be allowed to deflect attention from the point that it illustrated the difficulties facing any attempts to deal with the size and composition of the port registers and the emotions raised by any moves in such directions.

The Attitude of the Transport and General Workers' Union

The senior officials of the Transport and General Workers' Union were committed to the idea of something like the 1947 Dock Labour Scheme. They had campaigned for it during and immediately after the Second World War, and, to a large extent, its existence was a result of their pressure. This does not mean that the 1947 scheme was their "ideal": however, they believed it was a major improvement on past practice. In essence they took the view, in the final stages of the negotiations over the 1947 scheme, that they had to make concessions in order to get agreement. Some of these concessions, such as those on the issue of overtime, were made in the knowledge that they might be the cause of concern to their members, but in the belief that they were worth making in order that a workable scheme could be in reduced.

Once the 1947 scheme came into operation, officials of the Transport and General Workers' Union, including the General Secretary during the early postwar years, Arthur Deakin, were willing to press for changes, and for what they and their members saw as improvements. Earlier it was noted, for example, that Deakin gave an undertaking to press for changes in the disciplinary arrangements. Similarly, attempts were made to alter the provisions relating to overtime. However, Deakin was not willing to support industrial action to force through these changes if this meant that the employers could call the union's attachment to the scheme into question. In essence, the presentation of the scheme was the critical issue, and if necessary, the restrictions that some workers saw as "irksome" might just have to be lived with. This position was made clear on a number of different occasions.

For example, the Transport and General Workers' Union set up its own internal inquiry into the unofficial strike at Manchester. In the report of the committee of inquiry it was stated:

> ... it is to be noted that under the Dock Labour Scheme reasonable overtime working is obligatory and part of a port worker's conditions of employment, this is a "quid pro quo" for the advantages and benefits conferred by the Scheme when related to the conditions which operated prior to its introduction ...

> Irresponsible action of the character endorsed in connection with the unofficial strike cannot but prejudice the future of the Dock Labour Scheme which, admittedly, has completely revolutionised conditions in the Dock Industry. The Scheme accords great advantages and benefits compared with the conditions which operated prior to its introduction, but in return there must of necessity be obligations resting upon the port workers. In other words, the requirements of the Scheme must be observed and further, there must be a disciplined approach to any questions which may arise from time to time in connection with its operation. Failing this, we are convinced that in the final result the Scheme will be wrecked, with disastrous consequences to all concerned.[27]

When a dispute concerning overtime arose a number of years later, in 1954, the General Secretary of the Transport and General Workers' Union took the same line as with the Manchester strike. Thus, he said:

> The Dock Labour Scheme rests entirely upon our willingness to undertake work at all times when it is necessary in the Port Transport Industry, and any refusal to undertake overtime is a repudiation of our contractural obligations.[28]

In a report to the General Executive Council, attention was drawn to the dangers in any repudiation of obligations for the continuation of the Scheme.

> In the event of a prolongation of the (overtime) stoppage the question of the continuation or otherwise of the National Dock Labour Scheme would undoubtedly be brought under review.[29]

It was not just when overtime was at issue that this approach was taken. The line of argument was a familiar one for a whole range of issues. Thus, during the dock strikes at Avonmouth, Bristol, Liverpool and London in 1949 over the unloading of Canadian ships, the General Executive Council of the Transport and General Workers' Union passed the following resolution:"That the National Joint Council for the Dock Industry be informed that it is the policy of this Union to at all times accept and fulfil the responsibilities and obligations associated with the collective agreements in the Port Transport Industry and the Dock Workers (Regulation of Employment) Scheme."[30]

Similarly, in 1952, when considering the reduction in employment opportunities in the industry and the need to revise the register, the General Secretary said:

> One thing emerges quite clearly, the Register is carrying a far larger number of men than is necessary to handle the volume of work going through the ports at this time. We cannot escape the impact of this. In fact, unless we are prepared to recognise it and make a readjustment in the number of men employed, the Dock Labour Scheme may become the subject of serious challenge.[31]

It needs to be recognised, that while the leadership of the Transport and General Workers' Union knew that some of their members disliked the restrictions placed on them by the 1947 scheme, they took the view that, in fact, the extent of the restrictions was often overstated: it was agreed that the "restrictions were not more onerous than those experienced by many workers in other industries"[32]. Deakin took the view that much of the agitation against aspects of the scheme was not fuelled by the provisions of the scheme but by other factors: "according to Deakin's mind, whatever factors caused the dockers to act as they did were external to the scheme"[33]. The external factors that Deakin had in mind in this context were the influence of the Communist Party and their sympathisers. Deakin, like Bevin, fought against such influences both within the union and the industry. The statement made by Deakin at a press conference during an unofficial strike on Merseyside in 1951 is representative of the position he adopted. In this particular case he clearly sought to link the strike to the claimed communist sympathies of the organisers: "After exhibiting a document, which he alleged had emanated from the World Federation of Trade Unions, instructing communist "agent provocateurs" in methods of "creating unrest and training merchant ship crews to be released from capitalist authority", Mr Deakin added: "It is clear that this underground activity amongst seamen is going on amongst dockers too. The clear intention is to strike at countries which do not accept the communist outlook and at the point at wh ch they are most vulnerable".[34]

Of course, Deakin was not alone in expressing such views. From one point of view their accuracy does not matter. The important point is that Deakin seemed to believe them (certainly all of the evidence collected by a number of academics[35] suggested he did), and acted on this basis.

The other challenge that the leaders of the Transport and General Workers' Union came more directly from the employers over the question of joint control (the way joint control operated was also the source of discontent amongst some union members, but the employers opposed the principle of joint control as such). However, the union was not willing to contemplate the principle of joint control being abandoned. This was made perfectly clear in the union's evidence to the official inquiries that considered joint control, and in a bulletin produced by the Transport and General Workers' Union after the report of the Devlin Committee in 1956[36]. In this bulletin it was argued that:

> The attempt of the Port Employers to undermine the Scheme has been rejected. Certain amendments of a minor character are proposed, but in general principle the Committee has definitely come down in favour of the continuance of the scheme in its present form. This can be regarded as most satisfactory from our point of view; indeed it would have been little short of tragic if the Port Employers had succeeded in their attempt to virtually test control in themselves. The basic structure of the Scheme would have been destroyed with a return, eventually, to the position which existed prior to Ernest Bevin having this great conception.[37]

There is no reason to believe, though, that this was simply Deakin's own view: to the contrary, all the evidence suggests that this view was shared by all of the union's senior officials, and many others who held official positions. While it might be pointed out that in 1953 a resolution appeared on the agenda for the Biennial Delegate Conference that no permanent officials should be members of local dock labour boards, it is fair also to record that this resolution wa never formally proposed and seemed to have little support. Indeed joint control had always been seen by the Transport and General Workers' Union as central to any scheme to deal with casual employment, and in early discussions on registration the union had resisted any attempts to introduce schemes without such a provision.

Of course, the position of other unions and the unofficial movements was different. The Dock Labour Scheme offered the Transport and General Workers' Union a dominant position thereby potentially threatening those other organisations. It should be no surprise that they sought to exploit the problems in the industry to attach the position of the Transport and General Workers' Union and to try to gain the initiative.

The Attitude of Trade Union Members

Most trade union members, like the union leaders, recognised that the 1947 Dock Labour Scheme offered benefits. However, the benefits varied from worker to worker. Some who were sought after, maybe specialist workers, could secure high earnings and on most occasions, work when they wanted. Attendance money and guaranteed payments, certainly at the level on offer, meant little to them.

Possibly more important, though, most workers, even those that accepted there were some benefits to be gained from the scheme, also saw major disadvantages. In particular, they did not accept the restrictions that were also part of the scheme. For example, the Leggett report noted that under the provisions of the Scheme a man could no longer pick and choose from the work available as he had been able to do in the past. It said that there was "much resistance among some of the men to these limitations on freedom of choice ... In the case of some of the men, we believe that, because of the restrictions and limitations on freedom which it entails, the Scheme presents itself in some ways as a worsening rather than an improvement in their way of life."[38]

A similar point was made by a writer in the Times, in an attempt to explain the "zinc oxide strike".

> The men's decision to continue the strike, in spite of the reduction of the penalty on the 11 men, can be understood only if there is a realisation of the change in which the decasualisation scheme has brought about in the dockers' habits of work. They say that in the days of casual labour they were their own masters. They could exercise their own choice of job. If they fell out with one employer they could go to another. In a score of different ways they could influence their conditions.

Now, they say, there is only one employer. They must go wherever they are sent and if they rebel they are subject to a discipline from which they cannot escape. They feel themselves helpless in the grip of a monopoly which holds absolute power over their livelihood. If it is pointed out to them that there is the most carefully drawn up machinery for appeal to committees on which their union is strongly represented, they reply bluntly that the union cannot or does not defend them against the board and the employers.'[39]

It was feelings such as these that led dock workers to react against a number of specific provisions of the 1947 Dock Labour Scheme during the late 1940s and 1950s. However, they did not simply react against the Scheme, but they also reacted against their unions, in particular the Transport and General Workers' Union. They saw the union as being involved in both supporting the scheme in general and imposing some of the particular restrictions to which they objected. This belief was particularly visible from a number of the strikes during this period. For example, the Liverpool University research team that studied the Manchester dock strike noted that the dockers saved much of their hostility for their own union leaders who they believed were responsible for the action taken against the men.

> It is true that the day the strike started the Chairman of the Unofficial Committee had told the dock workers that they were fighting the shipowners, the Ship Canal Company (the main employer), the Dock Labour Board which was supporting the shipowners, and the trade union which was afraid of them all, but at the following meetings the speakers' targets had been the Area Labour Manager who suspended the men and the trade union officials who had accepted the employers' proposals about overtime and refused to take up the case. Except on one occasion when an unfounded rumour went round that the Company was threatening to discharge all foremen, little or no ill was shown towards it.[40]

This hostility towards the union spilt over from concern about specific provisions of the scheme to a more general antagonism. Thus, in 1951, when the unions agreed on a daily wage increase of two shillings a day for time workers (and corresponding increases for piece workers), dockers in a number of ports went on strike for what they termed the "Dockers' Charter". It was made clear during the strike, that much, if not most, antagonism was directed against the unions, in particular, the Transport and General Workers' Union, which refused to reopen negotiations with employers. When seven dock workers were arrested and brought to court, charged with organising the strikes in contravention of the Conditions of Employment and National Arbitration Order, their defending council said:

> The strike was not against collective bargaining but to secure it. It was ridiculous to suggest that this was a dispute between the men and the employers. If the union had

said that they would reopen negotiations with the employers the strike would not have lasted another ten minutes.[41]

One result of the degree of antagonism between dock workers and union leaders was the reduction in membership of the Transport and General Workers' Union in the industry. Of course, the reductions in membership that might be noted were not simply a result of this antagonism but also were partly a reflection of the reduction in the number of people employed in the industry. However, this latter factor alone cannot explain, for example, the reduction in membership of the Transport Workers' Union from 74,858 at the end of 1956 to 63,913 at the end of 1958. Such reductions, at least in part, were a reflection of the fact that some dockers were becoming disenchanted with the union and were transferring their allegiance, either to the unofficial movements or to one of the other unions operating in the industry.

The unofficial movements were established on the docks from the late 1940s. In London, for example, the unofficial committee which organised the "zinc oxide strike" maintained control throughout the conflict. Thus, when the strike ended, one commentator said:

> An unsatisfactory feature of the way the strike has ended is that the unofficial leaders, while they have not secured any kind of recognition outside, have kept their hold on the leadership till the end. They have succeeded in maintaining their control over the men throughout the strike, and it is they who have ordered the men back to work ... Some observers have concluded that there must be something wrong with the organisation or administration of the union.[42]

Earlier it was noted that when the strike ended, the unofficial committee did not disband as happens on most similar occasions, but continued to operate as an important and influential body for many years to come. Similar developments can be noted at most other major ports: and possibly more importantly, the unofficial committees in the different ports developed strong links. Thus, Allen said:

> Whenever a strike occurred in a port in the postwar period the permanent or semi-permanent unofficial port workers committee which organised it would dispatch envoys to other ports for support. The envoys became so accomplished in the art of strike spreading and rarely failed to secure an extension of the strike. Unofficial interport communications during disputes became an accepted procedure, and dockers would wait in anticipation of a call to strike whenever they heard men in another port were striking, or even contemplating strike action.[43]

In some ways, however, the problems facing the Transport and General Workers' Union over this period are better exemplified by the move made by the National Amalgamated Stevedores and Dockers union into ports which were traditionally a stronghold of the Transport and General Workers' Union. The Stevedores union had always claimed considerable support in London, but had not organised to any extent in the other major British ports. In August 1954, an unofficial dispute at the port of Hull over the discharge of grain, led a number of dockers to apply to join the Stevedores union. Over the next year, the Stevedores union recruited members in Merseyside and in Manchester as well. Events surrounding this development are complex, involving an investigation by the TUC's disputes committee[44], an interpretation of the Bridlington Agreement[45] and a celebrated court case[46]. However, from the point of view of this discussion, two points are crucial. First, the ostensible reason for the defection of members of the Transport and General Workers' Union to the Stevedores union was that the former union refused to give the unofficial strike at Hull official support. It is worthwhile recording that in the late 1940s and early 1950s, numerous strikes occurred in the port transport industry where not only did the Transport and General Workers' Union fail to give support, but also actively opposed the strike. This is not to argue that the unofficial strike, or the attitude adopted by the Transport union to previous unofficial strikes was the only cause of the defection. There had been a long history of conflict between the Transport and the Stevedores union, dating back to the original amalgamation which led to the formation of the Transport union, and including a "poaching dispute" in 1925 and the "ineffectives strike" in 1949. Nevertheless, the failure of the Transport union to support the Hull dockers confirmed the union's attitude towards unofficial action and towards dockers who would not accept the obligations of the Dock Labour Scheme and undoubtedly was a major factor in the defection.

The second important point to make about this development is that it led to a significant loss of membership from the docks section of the Transport and General Workers' Union. In the northern ports about 10,000 dockers transferred their allegiance from the Transport to the Stevedores union. Furthermore, although the precise number of members in the two unions is difficult to determine (there is some evidence that in a number of ports both unions lost members as a result of the conflict in later years[47]), the Stevedores union maintained a significant membership in northern ports and broke the Transport union's previous domination.

Notes

1. Ministry of Labour and National Service, *Report of a Committee to Inquire into the Operation of the Dock Workers (Regulation of Employment) Act 1946*, HMSO, London, 1946.
2. Ministry of Labour and National Service, *Report of a Committee to Inquire into the Operation of the Dock Workers (Regulation of Employment) Scheme, 1947*, HMSO, London, 1946, Cmnd 9831, p1.
3. *Ibid.*
4. *Ibid*, p90.
5. Barnard v National Dock Labour Board.
6. See report in Times, 3 June 1948, p4.
7. *Op Cit*, p33.
8. Ministry of Labour and National Service, *Unofficial Stoppages in the London Docks*, HMSO, London, 1951, p1.
9. *Ibid*, p26.
10. *Ibid*, p26.
11. *Ibid*, p43.
12. *Ibid*, p50.
13. Clause 85(b).
14. Meetings held in September 1950.
15. T S Simey, *The Dock Worker*, Liverpool University Press, Liverpool, 1956.
16. *Ibid.*
17. Ministry of Labour and National Service, *Report on Certain Aspects of the Manchester (Salford) Dock Strike, April-June 1951*, HMSO, London, 1951, Cmd 8375.
18. Ministry of Labour and National Service, *Final Report of a Court Inquiry into a Dispute in the London Docks*, HMSO, London, 1954.
19. Times, 30 October 1952, p5.
20. Times, 20 November 1952, p4.
21. Times, 21 July 1953, p5.

22.   Times, 14 April 1954, p4.23Times, 26 November 1954, p4.
24.   Times, 26 October 1956, p6.
25.   Times, 9 November 1956, p5.
26.   Keesings Contemporary Archives, April 1949, p9969.
27.   Transport and General Workers' Union, General Executive Council Minutes, Appendix II, 4 March 1952, pp 56-57.
28.   Transport and General Workers' Union General Secretary's Report to the General Executive Council, 1 March 1954, p56.
29.   Transport and General Workers' Union, General Secretary's Report to the General Executive Council, December 1954, p152.
30.   Transport and General Workers' Union, General Executive Council, Minute 575, 30 June 1949, p143.
31.   Transport and General Workers' Union, General Secretary's Report to the General Executive Council, 15 December 1952, p232.
32.   V C Allen, Trade Union Leadership, Longman, London, pp 204-205.
33.   *Ibid*, p205.
34.   Kenning's Contemporary Archives, 3 March 1951.
35.   See for example, V C Allen, *Op Cit*.
36.   *Op Cit*.
37.   Transport and General Workers' Union, General Secretary's Report to the General Executive Council, 17 September 1956, p168.
38.   *Op Cit*, p27.
39.   19 June 1948, p4.
40.   T S Simey, *Op Cit*, p242.
41.   R Heilbron, Defence Counsel for Merseyside Dockers, quoted in Times, 17 April 1951, p3.
42   Times, 30 June 1948, p4.
43.   *Op Cit*, pp 198-199.

6 Decasualisation of dock labour

The conflict in the port transport industry, particularly that relating to the operation of the 1947 Dock Labour Scheme, was not a phenomenon confined to the early post war years, but continued into the early 1960s. Strike activity in the industry was greater in the early 1960s than it has been in the late 1950s and a large proportion of strikes ostensibly were the result of disputes over the operation of the Dock Labour Scheme. For example, about 32 per cent of all "principal stoppages"[1] in the industry were apparently linked to unpopular decisions of the Dock Labour Board.

Disputes over the operation of the 1947 Scheme, however, did not lead the main unions or employers to consider abandoning the approach to the problem of casual employment which its provisions embodied: to the contrary, unions and employers agreed to reinforce this approach and move towards the decasualisation of dock labour.

1961 Directive on Decasualisation

The Leggett[2] and the 1956 Devlin[3] reports both had suggested that moves might be made to further regularise employment in the port transport industry. However, the real catalyst for the moves towards the decasualisation of dock labour was the evidence of conflict in the industry already referred to. Two major strikes occurred in the port of London, the first in September and October 1960, and the second in April and May of the following year. The first of these was a strike of tally clerks, which brought a large section of the trade of the port of London to a standstill for a month; the second condemned the use of non-registered labour for dock work and was rather less extensive, but still managed to seriously disrupt traffic in the port for two weeks. Both of the strikes were unofficial. They persuaded the port employers that new efforts had to be made to improve industrial elations in the industry and they enabled the Transport and General Workers' Union to press a case they had raised on a number of previous occasions. Following these strikes informal talks were held on ways of improving industrial relations in the industry, and the Transport and General Workers' Union pressed the case for decasualisation. Subsequently, these talks were continued on a more formal level through the National Joint Council for the Port Transport Industry, and, on 6 June 1961, the Council declared that a "further measure" of decasualisation was an essential prerequisite for the improvement of labour relations in the industry. Interestingly, the following day, when the General Secretary of the Transport and General Workers' Union reported to the General Executive Council, according to the minutes of that meeting, he did not mention the issue of decasualisation: he simply said that at a meeting of the National Joint Council discussion ensured, "during the course of which the Council noted the decision recorded to establish a Working Party to further examine the general question of industrial relations in the industry, and report"[4]. However, three months later when the General Secretary presented a further report, the importance of discussions on decasualisation was clearly spelt out: thus, the minutes of the meeting record that the General Secretary reported on the agreement with the employers "to set up a Working Party to examine ways and means of achieving a greater regularity of employment and better living standards for workpeople in the Port Transport Industry"[5].

The Working Party reported back to the National Joint Council later in 1961 and in October of that year, the Council issued a policy directive to all local joint committees instructing them to draw up schemes for decasualising dock labour in their own area. The directive laid down the principles on which any scheme for decasualisation should be based. These were:

1   The preservation of the 1947 Dock Labour Scheme;
2   The engagement of a majority of registered dock workers on a weekly basis;
3   The freedom of any worker to refuse the offer of a weekly engagement, even though after a reasonable period of service most dockers should expect to receive an offer of engagement on such terms;
4   Provision of "allocation by rotation" of men not engaged on a weekly basis;
5   The abolition of restrictive practices and encouragement of the mobility of labour;
6   The maximum possible use of mechanical aids;
7   The adoption of shift systems of working whenever possible.

Two aspects of this directive are particularly interesting. The first is that although decasualisation and weekly engagements were being pressed, it was recognised that some dockers did not seek such employment and it was insisted that they should be free to refuse it. The second is that decasualisation was not simply linked to improved industrial relations (or, more specifically, industrial conflict, as is the original agreement of the Working Party), but was also linked to ways of increasing "efficiency" in the industry. There is little doubt that the influential employers were persuaded that decasualisation could bring direct economic benefits to themselves as well as desirable social benefits for dock workers.

Local negotiations began on the irective in a number of ports almost immediately it was received. For example, in Liverpool, a special sub-committee was set up of three employers and three employee representatives in October 1961, and the sub-committee held its first meeting on 8 December of that year. However, in that port progress was delayed for more than a year because of the dispute between the Transport and General Workers' Union and the National Amalgamated Stevedores and Dockers union and the attempt of the former union to restrict any scheme to their members alone. Negotiations did not begin seriously until March 1963, and then only on the understanding that the question of whom any scheme would cover would be returned to at a later date.

In fact, once negotiations were underway seriously, they were brought to a swift conclusion. In September of 1963 the basis of a "decasualisation Scheme" was agreed. The Scheme provided for dock workers to be grouped into one of four different categories: "group A" which covered established contract workers, "group B" which covered company contract workers, "group C" which covered port contract workers, and "group D" which was the reserve pool. All workers in the first three groups were to be offered permanent employment, although workers in thelast group were to remain casual employees. It was estimated that on this basis only about ten per cent of the workforce of the port would remain as casual workers.

Although the scheme was agreed in September of 1963, it was not publicly launched until January of the following year, and then amid a blaze of publicity. However, the publicity, rather than persuading the rank and file docker to accept the scheme, worked in the opposite way: it was interpreted as an attempt to pressurise workers into accepting something against their own interests. In the end, the scheme was rejected by all branches of the Transport and General Workers' Union and the National Amalgamated Stevedores and Dockers union in the port.

The position in other ports differed in detail though there were many points of similarity. In Hull, for example, the interunion difficulties which had held up negotiations at Liverpool, managed to prevent any serious discussion at all. In Bristol, the issue of the percentage of the labour force that should be offered permanent employment, that had been raised at Liverpool through the categorisation of workers, was a matter of debate and prevented any real progress being made. The same problem arose in London: in addition, there was a dispute over whether the "terms of employment" (decasualisation) could be discussed separately from working conditions.

When the position was reviewed at a national level, these problems surfaced again: the employers and the unions disagreed, for example, on the proportion of the labour force and the number of ports that should be covered by any agreement (the Transport and General Workers' Union argued for complete coverage of both the workforce and the ports). In addition, as had happened in London, the employers began to demand firmer assurances that the costs of decasualisation would be compensated for by increased efficiency, assurances that the trade unions claimed were unnecessary. The result was that negotiations on the National Directive ground to a halt and it became clear that if further progress was to be made, then a new initiative would be needed.

Rochdale Report

While negotiations on the National Directive were taking place, a major report on the workings of Britain's ports was published. The report, published in September 1962, was the result of an inquiry under the chairmanship of Viscount Rochdale[6]. It was an extremely wide ranging document, concerned with all aspects of the operation of British ports, not simply dock labour. It dealt, for example, with items like containerisation, mechanisation and port ownership. However, it also dealt with the question of decasualisation.

The committee was aware that discussions were underway, both nationally and locally, on decasualisation, and they referred to these discussions in their report. In general they gave support to the view that had been expressed in the National Joint Committee Directive that a "further measure of decasualisation" was desirable. Thus, the report said:

> We support the National Joint Council for the Port Transport Industry in its view that decasualisation is the right approach to securing a more contented and efficient dock

labour force and we endorse the general principles it has laid down as a basis for implementing decasualisation proposals.[7]

However, the report did more than simply support the general view that the discussions embarked upon were desirable: it also commented on issues which were already becoming a matter of contention between the trade unions and the employers. For example, although the committee recognised that it was desirable that decasualisation should cover all workers and all ports, it argued that if such a comprehensive, national scheme was not possible, a more partial solution should be seriously examined. Similarly, the committee report stressed the importance of decasualisation being accompanied by an improvement in efficiency: thus, "greater efficiency should be a result of decasualisation, indeed it must be a condition of it"[8].

In practice, the report of the Rochdale Committee received a mixed reception, not simply on the issue of decasualisation. A number of the central recommendations of the report on the control and coordination of ports were not accepted[9], and on the specific question of decasualisation, the report served to do little other than highlight existing disagreements.

The Devlin Committee

It is argued, then, that the negotiations on decasualisation, as a result of the National Directive, achieved little of permanent value, and the report of the Rochdale Committee did little more than exemplify thedifferences between the unions and the employers over crucial issues. However, these and other attempts to initiate discussion on decasualisation in the early 1960s should not be dismissed as unimportant: not only did they illustrate the desire for change on the part of a number of different interest groups, but they also provided essential background discussion. Nevertheless, the decasualisation of dock labour was not the direct result of such matters: the direct link was provided by the report of another official inquiry into labour relations in the industry, the report of a committee chaired by Lord Devlin[10].

The Devlin Committee was set up in October 1964, following the breakdown of talks over a wage increase. The trade unions had demanded a wage increase of £1 5s a week for time workers and of five per cent for piece workers; in their last offer the employers had offered 12s 6d a week for time workers, three and a half per cent for piece workers and an increase in fallback pay from £7 16s to £9 a week. A dockers' delegate conference had rejected the employers' last offer, even as an interim measure, and the unions had formally given four weeks' notice of their intention to strike.

The Devlin Committee was asked to inquire into three matters: first, "the causes and circumstances of the present dispute"; second, "decasualisation"; and, third, "causes of dissension in the industry and other matters affecting efficiency of working"[11]. In practice, the second and third matters were treated together by the committee and dealt with in the final report published in July 1965[12]: the first matter, the wages dispute, was dealt with separately in an interim report publishedin November 1964[13] (it recommended a wage increase of 19s 2d a week for time workers and five per cent for piece workers).

The committee's main report was a wide-ranging document which thoroughly examined the history of labour relations in the port transport industry, particularly since the introduction of the 1947 Dock Labour Scheme. It highlighted nine main causes of dissension and inefficiency:

1   The dockers' irregular pattern of employment and earnings;
2   The preferential treatment shown to some dockers who were offered regular work, when others were not;
3   The dockers' lack of responsibility;

4   Deficiencies of management, especially amongst the many casual employers;
5   Time-wasting practices;
6   Piecework;
7   Overtime provisions;
8   Inadequate welfare amenities and working conditions;
9   Trade union problems.

However, throughout the discussion one main theme dominated: the central problem was that of the casual system of employment. For example, when discussing the dockers' "lack of responsibility", the committee said:

It would indeed be surprising if the casual system of employment in the docks did not produce a more irresponsible attitude than that in industry generally. Casual labour produces a casual attitude. If the employer does not provide work unless he wants to, why should the employee go to work unless he wants to? If a man is used to having work one day and none the next, is there anything very wrong about taking a day off of his own choice, whether for his own pleasure or to air a grievance by a token strike?[14]

A similar, if less direct point, was made when discussing the problem arising from the overtime provisions:

It cannot be suggested that difficulties over overtime and weekend working are directly due to the casual system, but it can be said that under conditions of normal and regular employment they would be less likely to be pushed to the point of dissension.[15]

It came as no surprise, therefore, when the committee concluded their report by recommending that action be taken effectively to eliminate the use of casual employment on the docks. It suggested that all men should be offered engagement on a weekly basis (although provisions were outlined for worksharing and the temporary transfer of men between employers). It was also argued that in parallel with the elimination of casual employment, moves should be made to eliminate the casual employer from the industry.

The committee argued that decasualisation would not simply be a reform of social benefit, but would also be one which would help to reduce dissension and inefficiency. However, in a recommendation which commented directly on the debate between the two sides of industry following the National Directive, it is suggested that negotiations on any specific reforms on, for example, working practices, which did not necessarily flow from decasualisation, should await a later second stage.

Moves Towards Decasualisation

The report of the Devlin Committee was welcomed by both sides of the National Joint Council for the industry, and, following its publication, the Council set up the National Modernisation Committee (composed of six representatives from each side of industry, with the National Amalgamated Stevedores and Dockers' union supplying part of the representation for the employees' side, and four independent members, one of whom, Lord Brown, acted as chairman). The committee was able to reach agreement on the major points relatively quickly, and in March 1966, the Minister of Labour published a draft order giving effect to their proposals.

The draft order invited objections to the proposals and these were considered at an inquiry conducted by Sir George Honeyman[16]. The inquiry considered objections concerning the inclusion of ports, the contributions and powers of the dock labour boards, joint control and the structure of the industry. In practice, the inquiry recommended few major changes to the draft order. For example, it rejected claims for both widening and reducing the range of ports to be covered by the scheme, and it argued that the question of the structure of the industry was outside its terms of reference. One question of detail on which it did declare a view, which was of some significance, was the membership of the dock labour boards. It agreed with the objection of the National Amalgamated Stevedores and Dockers' union that membership should not be restricted to unions represented on local joint committees (the Stevedores union itself was not represented on most joint committees), and suggested instead that anybody that was party to an agreement recognised by the National Joint Council should have the right to be nominated for a local board.

The level of pay to accompany decasualisation was not considered by the Honeyman inquiry: instead the Devlin Committee was reconvened[17]. The committee broadly accepted that the levels of renumeration suggested by the employers would be reasonable. As a result it suggested that a "modernisation payment" (a flat rate bonus) of 1s an hour should be paid to all dockers, and that the weekly guarantee should be increased to £15: in total, their proposals represented an increase in the wages bill of about 16 per cent.

The scheme for the decasualisation of dock labour was introduced through the Docks and Harbo rs Act of 1966 and the Dock Labour Order of 1967. The 1966 Act was concerned centrally with the decasualisation of employers, whereas the 1967 Order was concerned primarily with the decasualisation of dock workers. Under the Act licensing authorities were established. These authorities had the right to determine who could and who could not act as an employer on the docks, and in reaching their decision they had to take account of the ability of the employer to offer permanent employment to dock workers. In the event the number of employers operating on the docks was substantially reduced: prior to decasualisation there had been over 1,200 employers in registered ports, whereas afterwards the number was around 500.

The 1967 Order did not change the essential framework established for controlling labour in the industry by the 1947 Dock Labour Scheme. The system of dock labour boards was retained, and the boards kept their overall responsibilities for recruitment and discipline[18]. The crucial change brought about by the 1967 Order related to the terms of employment. Three different categories of dock workers were established: the "permanent worker" who was to be employed under a contract of service which required not less than one weeks' notice fortermination by either side, the "supplementary worker" who was to be registered for a limited period only, often simply for the completion of a particular task, and the "temporarily unattached worker", a fully registered dock worker who had been unable to obtain permanent employment and would be under the control of, and employed by, the National Dock Labour Board. It was made clear that it was anticipated that a worker would only remain in the temporarily unattached category for a short period of time: otherwise, in effect, a proportion of the workforce would have been casual employees, and if this proportion had been significant, then it would have been difficult to claim that dock work had been decasualised. In fact, this issue was to cause major problems and further provisions had to be agreed on this matter[19]

Attitude of the Unions

The Transport and General Workers' Union had fought for the introduction of the 1947 Dock Labour Scheme and fought for the retention of its central principles in later years. However, officials of the unions, it has been noted earlier, were never happy with every detail of the scheme, and during the 1950s many came to believe that major changes were necessary. The changes they believed to be necessary were not those suggested by the employers (such as the abandoning of joint control) but were concerned with the basis of employment practices in the industry. The National Docks Secretary, O'Leary, expressed such views in a trade group review.

> The principle of decasualisation for the industry was first laid down in 1920, and with the coming into being of the Dock LabourScheme it was felt that a very real step forward in this direction had been made. The existing Scheme, however, has been in operation since 1947 and we are still faced with the problem of how to remove the curse of casual employment that still obtains in the docks. This continues to be the really basic question for our industry - that there is no guarantee that a man going to the docks on any morning will, in fact, be going to work.[20]

By this time the union had also decided how it wanted the change in employment practices to be brought about. It demanded the complete decasualisation of labour in the industry, opposing any moves to seek its gradual elimination. In fact, union officers argued that the gradual, rather than complete, elimination of casual employment, was making conditions in the industry worse rather than better. Thus, in an article in the union's journal, it was stated:

> We have many difficult domestic problems, perhaps the greatest being that the authority of the "Board" to control the employment of portworkers has been gradually sabotaged by the extension of permanency. The labour force has been divided into two sections, "permanent labour" and "pool labour" creating an aristocratic system where in boom conditions the permanent men get the best of the work and in depressed conditions, all of the work; a development which was not envisaged by the architects of the "Scheme" and is alien to the principles of trade unionism. The danger which has arisen from this development is that employers have taken a big step towards achieving their declared aim of sole control of the labour force, for the only real control the "Board" exercises over the permanent labour is that employers have to pay a (reduced) levy for the men they employ permanently.[21]

The Transport and General Workers' Union's views on gradualism held up progress for the latter part of the 1950s and the early 1960s. In the late 1950s, it meant that the points made by official reports that further changes in employment practices might be desirable were never followed up, and in the early 1960s it was one of the factors that divided the two sides in the discussions over the National Joint Council Directive.

The union's case found favour with the Devlin Committee, and although the union did not accept everything suggested in the 1965 report, the views expressed in that report broadly were seen to be in line with thinking in the union. However, it is important to record that on one issue the union was far from united. This was the question of the importance of nationalisation for the industry, and whether this should be seen as a precondition or a further development of de asualisation.

When it became clear that decasualisation was likely to be recommended by the Devlin Committee, sections of the Transport and General Workers' Union began pressing for nationalisation to be considered at the same time. Early in 1965, a resolution to this effect was passed by Region No 1 and forwarded to the General Executive Council for consideration[22]. In the event, the regional representative agreed that the resolution should be referred: nevertheless, the issue continued to be an important source of debate with the Biennial Delegate Conference accepting the principle of an extension of public ownership. There was no doubt widespread support within the union for the nationalisation of the industry, support which, as Jack Jones pointed out[23], was shared by the national officers. However, there was not such unanimity on the question of priorities. The national officials made it clear that they believed that the union must accept decasualisation as an important reform in its own right and must not insist on nationalisation of the industry as a prior condition. This was made clear by the National Secretary for the Docks group, O'Leary. He said:

> During the negotiations on decasualisation, the Workers' side of the industry has considered the question of nationalisation. It is their view that, although they believe in nationalisation of theport transport industry, the government's policy might not be put into operation for some time to come; therefore, they decided that they should go ahead with their efforts to obtain a scheme for Decasualisation for the docks industry. In the opinion of the workers' side for the National Joint Council for the Port Transport Industry, this would provide a better basis on which nationalisation could be built.[24]

The question of priorities is one which might be extended further. It is clear that decasualisation was not simply afforded a level of priority that mean it could be implemented ahead of nationalisation; it was also afforded a level of priority which meant that problems of working arrangements and the like had to be accepted so that the opportunity of decasualisation was not missed. In other words, decasualisation was a major priority and dockers might have to accept practice in other areas with which they and their union officials might disagree, in order that it could be introduced. Thus, when problems and disputes arose over the introduction of decasualisation, the General Executive Council issued a statement saying:

> The Council ... recognises that there are many personal problems of allocation and sharing of work that inevitably arise in a change of this size, but emphasises that these issues must be settled, as many have already, through the negotiating machinery ... Great opportunities for improving the livelihood and security of port workers now lie ahead. The union is determined to achieve these aims ...[25]

Attitudes of Dock Workers

There is little doubt that many members shared the enthusiasm shown by national union officials for decasualisation. The decasualisation proposals were fully discussed at various levels in the Transport and General Workers' Union and, at the end of the day, votes in favour of the line pursued were secured. Over some issues there was little disagreement, even during discussion. For example, there was widespread support for the rejection of the employers' proposals for a gradual introduction of decasualisation. In Hull, dockers held a series of one-day strikes early in 1961, in protest against the employers' proposals and succeeded in reversing the gradual increase in the number of permanent positions (the employers agreed to reduce the proportion of permanent positions from 40 to 35 per cent).

However, the policy adopted by the Transport and General Workers' Union was not always as widely supported. In two instances, dockers rejected proposals for decasualisation linked to the 1961 directive after they had been accepted by union leaders. In one instance, that of the London tally clerks, the position was complicated and the precise feelings of the men are difficult to discuss. A scheme for 100 per cent decasualisation was agreed between the Transport and General Workers' Union and the employers, and endorsed at a meeting of some 600 members in October 1964. The position of tally clerks who were members of the Stevedores union was less clear, and in the following month a number of branches voted against the proposals. The Transport and General Workers' Union's leaders were prepared to sign an agreement on their own but such a strategy was eventually rejected by a mass meeting of tally clerks held in February 1965[26], even though by that time over two-thirds of all clerks had accepted contracts under the new scheme. The second instance, at Liverpool, was more clear cut. The details of the proposals drawn up for decasualisation at Liverpool under the terms of the 1961 Directive were outlined earlier, as was the fact that it was rejected by the membership. It is worthwhile recording, though, that despite that fact that it had been rejected by all of the Transport and General Workers' Union's branches in the port, the District Secretary and the District Committee never officially rejected the scheme, and in their negotiations with the employers asked simply that it should be allowed to "lie on the table"[27].

There was similar, fairly widespread, disagreement amongst dockers when the Devlin Committee's proposals were put forward. Although the official committees of the Transport and General Workers' Union accepted the proposals, as in earlier periods, many members were more sceptical of the benefits. Their scepticism arose for a number of different reasons, but none differed greatly from those heard before. One was the realisation that decasualisation would reduce their freedom to choose where, if not when, to work. This point was made by a number of commentators at the time. One noted that "one big consolation (of casual employment) was the flexibility of the system"[28]. Another commented that with decasualisation dockers would "lose the freedom of freelance, a casual existence which in many cases brings substantially higher rewards than unskilled labour could expect from elsewhere"[29]. This comment was echoed in another which stated that "many dockers actually prefer the casual systems; they like the sense of freedom that it gives them not to work from time to time, and also a good deal of choice, which they can exercise in various ways of the work they will do or the employer they will work for"[30].

Another reason for the scepticism of the dockers was the fear that it would bring an end to the "continuity rule" which provided that a docker had the right to complete a job he had begun. The rule offered adegree of security of employment valued by many workers (apparently valued, even though permanent employment was meant to offer greater security). Thus one docker was reported as having said: "The continuity rule is the greatest thing that has every happened to dock life. It gives you security. Take it away and you take away security"[31].

In addition to these factors, dockers also feared that "modernisation" would lead to redundancy (despite the guarantees to the contrary) and many believed that decasualisation should be accompanied by nationalisation. In this latter instance they had the support of other trade unions and groups operating in the docks, and some sections of the Transport and General Workers' Union.

The Transport and General Workers' Union, and its officers, were aware of this scepticism and the fears of many dockers. Nevertheless, they believed that decasualisation was so important that it had to be pursued, and members has to be persuaded to accept it. Thus, writing in the official journal of the union, the national docks officer said:

> A troublesome point is that in some ports some of our members may be content to stay as they are and, therefore, be reluctant to change. Our responsibility, however, is to improve the status and lot of all the men we represent. This is an important challenge of principle to us. Should our own people choose not to accept it will be very difficult to go back again to the employer about the casual conditions of employment in the industry.[32]

As has been noted, in the event, the union leaders persuaded the representatives on the official decision making bodies in the union to accept the decasualisation proposals. However, they failed to allay the fears of many dockers.

The introduction of decasualisation in September 1967 was accompanied by strike action in most of Britain's main ports. The precise issue differed, but all strikes were directly linked to decasualisation and reflected many of the fears discussed above. For example, in London, the strike occurred over the issue of the "continuity rule", while at Liverpool the strike occurred over wages and the effect that decasualisation would have on them (for instance, it was felt, a d a later official inquiry[33] accepted correctly, that the abolition of "welting", a practice by which only half the gang works at any one time, would result in a reduction of earnings). The strikes in some ports were settled quickly but in Liverpool they lasted for over a month.

The strikes were supported in some instances by other unions, and in virtually all instances by the unofficial movements. There was strong opposition by the unofficial movements to the decasualisation was introduced. They had campaigned, along with many rank and file dockers, for decasualisation only to be introduced along with nationalisation, and they continued their campaign throughout 1967. Their argument was that decasualisation on its own would strengthen the employers' hands, and, as a result, hinder the campaign for nationalisation. An article in the "Humberside Voice", a publication distributed widely amongst dockers in Hull, said that there was a "contradiction between the promise of nationalisation, and pressing ahead with the Devlin proposals, which actually strengthened the position of the private employers in the industry"[34]. It was also suggested that decasualisation would lead to redundancies because it was linked to "modernisation" and reduced employment opportunities. In this context it was pointed out that the employers had asked for £2 $^3/_4$ million to finance redundancies (although this was requested for voluntary, not compulsory, redundancies). The unofficial movements were also able to argue that decasualisation could lead to a reduction of earnings[35], a point which they made in support of some of the strikes that accompanied decasualisation.

Of course, in the event, such opposition failed to prevent the introduction of the scheme of decasualisation. This particular series of strikes were settled, with varying degrees of success for the strikers. However, some of the issues raised during the strikes reappeared subsequently, and strike activity continued at a high level (and in some areas increased) in the years following decasualisation[36].

Notes

1. Quoted in Ministry of Labour, *Final Report of the Committee of Inquiry into Certain Matters Concerning the Port Transport Industry*, HMSO, London, 1965, Cmnd 2734, at p5.
2. Ministry of Labour and National Service, *Unofficial Stoppages in the London Docks*, HMSO, London, 1951.
3. Ministry of Labour and National Service, *Report of a Committee to Inquire into the Operation of the Dock Workers (Regulation of Employment) Scheme, 1947*, HMSO, London, 1956, Cmnd 9831.
4. Transport and General Workers' Union, General Executive Council Minutes, 7 June 1961, minute 408, p108.
5. Transport and General Workers' Union, General Executive Council Minutes, 19 September 1961, minute 648, p167.
6. Ministry of Transport, *Report of a Committee of Inquiry into the Major Ports of Great Britain*, HMSO, London, 1962, Cmnd 1824.
7. Ibid, para 404.
8. Ibid, para 393.
9. For example, its recommendation that a National Ports Authority should be set up was

not accepted. Instead the National Ports Council with more limited powers was established.

10   The committee produced two reports: Ministry of Labour, *First Report of the Committee of Inquiry into Certain Matters Concerning the Port Transport Industry*, HMSO, London, 1964, Cmnd 2523; Ministry of Labour, *Final Report of the Committee of Inquiry into Certain Matters Concerning the Port Transport Industry*, HMSO, London, 1965, Cmnd 2734.

11   Ministry of Labour, 1965, Ibid, terms of reference of the committee reported in pp (ii).

12   Ibid

13   Ministry of Labour, Op Cit.

14   Ministry of Labour, 1965, Op Cit, p8.

15   Ibid, p29.

16   Ministry of Labour, Report of Inquiry held under Para 5 of the Schedule to the Dock Workers (Regulation of Employment) Act 1946, HMSO, London, 1966.

17   Ministry of Labour, *Report of the Committee of Inquiry into the Wages Structure and Level of Pay for Dock Workers*, HMSO, London, 1966, Cmnd 3104.

18   There were some minor changes, for example, in the area of discipline. Essentially, though, the broad outline of the system of dock labour boards established in 1947 was retained.

19   This issue became complicated by discussions on mechanisation and containerisation, and the designation of dock work.

20   Transport and General Workers' Union, Annual Review and Trade Group Report 1961/2, p70.

21   Record, December, 1961, p4, article by D Connolly.

22   Transport and General Workers' Union, General Executive Council, Minutes, 4 March 1965, minute 230.

23   Record, February, 1966, pp 3-5.

24   Transport and General Workers' Union Annual Review and Trade Group Report 1965/6, p76.

25   Transport and General Workers' Union, General Executive Council, 19 September 1967, minute 669.

26   Only 420 Transport and General Workers' Union clerks attended.

27   The scheme was prepared by the District Secretary without general discussion and the Devlin Report referred to the excessive secrecy surrounding the discussions.

28   V Ellenger, The Engine that Drives the System, *New Society*, 25 March 1965, p10.

29   J Graham, New Status in Old Docks, *Statist*, 1 March 1963, p639.

30   D Perkins, What's Wrong in the Docks, *Listener*, 23 June 1966, p895.

31   J Bulger, Devlin: How the Dockers Revolt, *New Society*, 12 August 1965, p18.

32   Record, March 1962, p5.

33   Ministry of Labour, *Report of Inquiry into the locally determined aspects of the system of payment and earnings opportunities of registered dock workers in the port of Liverpool (including Birkenhead)*, HMSO, London, 1967.

34   Humberside Voice, October 1968, p3.

35   Casual employment offered dockers the opportunity to move from job to job to get the highest possible earnings.

36   In 1968 there were 193 stoppages leading to a loss of 114,000 working days, and in 1969 there were 368 stoppages leading to a loss of

7 The development of a policy on decasualisation

It could reasonably be argued that the moves to decasualise dock labour were not simply supported but were enthusiastically pursued by the Transport and General Workers' Union over a period of more than 40 years. At times it was the union that pushed for and initiated discussion on decasualisation, and whenever the opportunity arose to enter into discussions on such matters with employers or governments, it was seized eagerly. For example, in the interwar years, the Transport and General Workers' Union played an important role in ensuring that registration and maintenance kept being brought back onto the agenda. In 1924, the union was able to link discussion of registration and maintenance with the settlement of a wages dispute and this led to the establishment of the Maclean Committee[1]: it also sought, on a number of occasions, to link the issue of maintenance to the review of unemployment insurance in the 1930s[2]. Similarly, Allen has noted that although there were many reasons for the introduction of the Dock Labour Scheme in 1947, "peacetime decasualisation could have been delayed, perhaps gone by default, had not the official pressure of the Union been constantly exerted to bring it about"[3].

In fact, decasualisation was almost an article of faith within the union. The benefits and drawback were never seriously debated at the national level. At times issues were raised (for example in 1953, the issue of joint control was the subject of a resolution to the Biennial Delegate Conference, but in fact, the resolution was never formally proposed) and decasualisation's place on a list of priorities was debated (for example, at the time when the 1965 Devlin report[4] was being reviewed in the Union there was some discussion about whether decasualisation should be sought ahead of, or at the same time as, nationalisation) yet such discussion rarely examined the desirability of decasualisation "per se"[5], and in the analysis of priorities, most of the union's national leaders consistently argued for decasualisation to be given the highest rating. This was the case, for example, during the Second World War when Bevin persuaded dockers to withdraw the "rule book", and in the late 1940s and early 1950s when the union's national leaders argued that sacrifices had to be made in other areas, and, what in other circumstances would have been unacceptable provisions, had to be adhered to, so as to ensure that external critics were given no reason to attack the 1947 Dock Labour Scheme.

The reasons for this "attachment" to the ideal of decasualisation are not hard to find. The union was formed at the time of the Shaw Inquiry[6], an event which brought decasualisation and Ernest Bevin, to national prominence. There is little doubt that Bevin had been firmly committed to decasualisation for many years prior to the Shaw Inquiry: he had seen moves towards decasualisation as a way of overcoming the poverty and demoralisation he had witnessed on the docks[7]. Initially influenced by colleagues like Dan Hill, he was one of the architects of the first registration scheme in Bristol. He was convinced that decasualisation would bring major benefits to dock workers. Nevertheless, as Bullock records[8], the Shaw Inquiry was a "turning point in Bevin's career, perhaps the most important of all". Through the Shaw Inquiry he became identified not simply with the dockers, but also with moves to alleviate the problems resulting from casual employment, and he in turn identified the union with this cause.

As his biographers have noted, Bevin was always careful to carry his national executive with him. He dominated the union because of his ability and personality. He did not simply tell his fellow union officials what policy would be adopted but he persuaded them of this view. As Evans noted, this does not mean that Bevin was unwilling to lead: it means that he was careful to take others with him.

> Bevin discovered fairly early in his career that leaders must be prepared to lead and not be content merely to levy the decisions of a committee. His skill in judging what the majority of his followers wanted, gave him confidence in asserting himself. This led to many accusations of dictatorship. But whenever he was challenged on this ground, he was always able to produce the authority of his executive council an assembly of working men who formed the supreme policymaking body of his union, for all his actions.[9]

In practice, of course, many of the national leadership already were personally committed to decasualisation and needed little persuading about its benefits. For example, it has been noted that a number of the national union leaders during and immediately after the Second World War strongly supported decasualisation: in particular Donovan, the national docks officer, and Harry Edwards, a chairman of the Union. Bevin, however, was able to persuade waverers of its central importance and ensured that the union spared no effort when making moves in this direction. Of course, his stature in the trade union movement, and his crucial role in bringing about the amalgamations that led to the formation of the Transport and General Workers' Union helped considerably in this respect.Bevin joined the government during the Second World War and eventually relinquished the leadership of the Transport and General Workers' Union. However, Bevin's influence extended well beyond his formal term of office. While in government he was a major figure in the labour movement in general, but more specifically, was in close contact with his own union. He also strongly influenced his successor in the Union. Deakin had no direct association with dock workers and "learnt" from Bevin about the dock workers' problems and their solutions. In particular, Deakin took Bevin's ideas on decasualisation on board and was a major figure in the negotiations for the 1947 Dock Labour Scheme: one commentator noted he claimed the scheme as his own handiwork[10].

Throughout the 1950s and early 1960s, the Transport and General Workers' Union national leadership reaffirmed its support for earlier policy decisions. They strongly opposed moves, for example, to alter one of the central features of the 1947 Dock Labour Scheme, "joint control". Again, it is important to stress that though (as indicated earlier) an attempt was made to debate joint control, that debate never took place. The policy on joint control was taken almost as a "given" by many union leaders, having its origins in the early registration schemes. The Transport and General Workers' Union, by the 1950s, was identified with joint control, and its defence of the principle was taken as an "accepted fact".

The emergence of Jack Jones to senior positions within the union and ultimately to the General Secretaryship was an important development, for he was the first national "leader" of the union to be closely identified with dock workers since Bevin (he had been a dock worker at the port of Liverpool). His support for the policy of decasualisation was crucial and he was able to reinforce the traditions of the union in this respect.

It is less easy to talk about the reactions of dock union members to the moves to decasualise dock labour in as straightforward a fashion as it has been to describe the policy of the Transport and General Workers' Union. The docks membership of the union did not simply change over time, but also contained numerous different groups and section. There were clear differences in member reaction, for example, in different ports. The enduring opposition of dock workers in the Scottish ports (particularly, but certainly not exclusively, Glasgow) to schemes of registration has been noted. This opposition dated back to the attempt to introduce the first registration scheme in Glasgow in 1912 and endured until the Second World War period. Even then, Glasgow dockers only accepted registration on a trial basis after a government ultimatum. At Aberdeen, dockers adopted a similar stance in the 1930s. In part, the opposition to registration was based on the extent of existing union control over working practices, which influenced dockers' perceptions of the benefits likely to be gained from registration. Similarly, there were differences in member reaction in terms of differences in employment status. Particular groups had been recognised as specialists and had been able to reserve certain types of work to themselves. This often meant that they were able to gain more regular and higher paid employment. Decasualisation, then, offered them relatively few benefits but might result in them having to accept work they would not have undertaken before. In such circumstances it should not be surprising that they were particularly suspicious of decasualisation and restrictions it might impose on them.

In trying to explain the support of the Transport and General Workers' Union for the policy of decasualisation, the importance of the role of its leaders, their personal attachment to it and their belief that it would bring major benefits to the dock worker, then, cannot be overstated. At the same time, one also has to recognise another factor. The Transport union saw, particularly in registration and maintenance, and then later the Dock Labour Scheme, a mechanism for increasing its hold over the industry. Many of the early schemes sought to link registration to union membership and registration thus could be a way of moving towards a closed shop where one did not exist, or reinforcing it where it existed already. This helps to explain why the unions were so keen in the early years to ensure that the schemes, at worst, were jointly controlled. The concern about government intervention and compulsion in the early schemes was that they might weaken union control of the register. Later, with the Dock Labour Scheme, a statutory basis was accepted but joint control was insisted upon, very clearly against the wishes of the dock employers.

The unions, though, sought to use registration not only as a way of strengthening their position with regard to nonmembers, but individual unions also sought to use it to strengthen their position with regard to competitors. Before the amalgamations which brought about the Transport and General Workers' Union the different dockers unions, like the National Union of Dock Labourers and the Dock, Wharf, River and General Workers' Union, fought for supremacy in the different ports, while, after the amalgamation, the Transport and General Workers' Union fought against some of the specialist unions which claimed dockers' allegiances. The ability to restrict registration to their own members offered unions major advantages, and the ability of a union to claim the right to all the seats on a joint body gave them a major weapon in their fight with competitors. In fact, the very reasons for the Transport and General Workers' Union support for decasualisation schemes provided the motive for other unions to oppose them. In particular, the National Amalgamated Stevedores and Dockers saw the Dock Labour Scheme as a device that the Transport Workers were using in an attempt to reinforce their hold on the industry and needed no more reason than that to be concerned about it. It has been noted that in Liverpool, following the 1961 Directive on Decasualisation, the negotiations on a local scheme were held up for over a year because of the attempt of the Transport and General Workers' Union to restrict any scheme to their members alone.

Some of the policies on decasualisation also had the effect of splitting dock workers and leading different groups to adopt different postures. A particularly good illustration of this is the attempt that was made on a number of occasions by the employers to increase the proportion of workers on permanent contracts. Such moves were opposed by the Transport and General Workers' Union because while it would have meant better employment prospects for some of their members, it would have meant even less stable conditions for others. The union recognised that these moves would split the membership. Different reactions as a result of differences in self interest could be anticipated and had to be guarded against. It is also likely, though the evidence on this matter is more difficult to obtain, that workers of different ages had different views of decasualisation and its probable benefits. Studies in other industries[11] have noted that frequently younger workers view casual employment as having a number of attractions: it allows them to move between jobs and maximise earnings, and it gives them greater freedom to decide their own work patterns. On the other hand, older workers are less likely to be able to take advantage of the situation in the fashion of their younger colleagues. They may be less attractive to employers (especially when, as with dock work, we are discussing a manual occupation) and the conditions which enable young workers the freedom to determine their own work patterns may simply result in older workers having fewer opportunities to work at all.

It is important, then, not to try to generalise too much about the attitude of dock union members towards decasualisation. Nevertheless, it can be noted that a various times, and in a number of different ports, the majority of dock workers lent their support to protests about the proposed direction of "reform" or policies that have been imposed. The example of Glasgow has already been referred to on a number of occasions and it has been made clear that for much of the period under discussion dockers at Glasgow were unwilling to accept schemes of registration. The evidence for such a statement has not been simply the numerous manifestations of conflict in that port, but also, in a number of instances, specially arranged polls designed to test opinion on particular registration schemes. Similarly, it is clear that at a number of English ports a sizeable proportion of dock workers placed the maintenance of the 1947 Dock Labour Schemes lower in a list of priorities than was the case with National leaders of the Transport and General Workers' Union, and were less willing to accept the restrictions that it imposed. Whether in particular cases a majority of dockers, or simply a sizeable minority, held such views is impossible to say: however, in a number of instances, a majority were willing to back action designed to oppose union policy.

Throughout the post Second World War period there were skirmishes, and in some cases, outright conflict, between the dock union membership and the national leadership of the Transport and General Workers' Union. This was probably most visible in the late 1940s and 1950s when in a number of cases unofficial strikes were directed as much against the union leadership as they were against the employers. Reference has been made, for example, to the fact that at the time of the Manchester (Salford) dock strike in 1951, many dockers at that port "blamed" their own union officials for the grievance at issue ("compulsory overtime") rather than the employer, the Manchester Ship Canal Company.

It would be wrong to argue that the disagreements referred to between the membership and the national leadership of the Transport and General Workers' Union in the post Second World War period simply were a reflection of the union's policy on decasualisation. Much more was involved, including in the first part of the period, the political orientation of the national union leadership. Nevertheless, it would be wrong also not to recognise that in some instances the union's policy on decasualisation played a part. In some cases it was simply that to dock workers the union leadership seemed to have its priorities wrong: in other cases, the participation of union leaders on bodies disciplining workers led members to believe that some union officials were not backing them to the extent they would have wished, and, as a result, this drove a wedge between union leaders and members.

However, in some ways the most significant indicator of dissent within the Transport and General Workers' Union, was the development of breakaway organisations and movements. Reference could be made, for example, to the establishment of the Scottish Transport and General Workers' Union, or to the development of a strong and semi-permanent unofficial movement linking many British ports, or to the extension of the National Amalgamated Stevedores and Dockers union from their London base to Northern ports. Again, it should be stressed that in none of these cases can it be claimed that the Transport and General Workers' Union's policy on decasualisation was the only reason for the development. In the case of the Scottish breakaway, the debate over the right to appoint officials and the traditional autonomy of Scottish branches undoubtedly was an important factor: in the case of the unofficial movement and the extension of the Stevedores union, personal disputes, and the more general approach of the union to industrial and political matters, needs to be taken into account. Nevertheless, the Transport and General Workers' Union's policy on decasualisation was also an important factor in all cases: it attracted criticism in its own right and contributed to the more general dissatisfaction on the part of some members with the conduct of the union's affairs. Even where it was not the only issue, it was a convenient one for the competing organisations to use to hang criticisms of the Transport and General Workers' Union on. It allowed those other organisations to claim that the Transport union was not properly defending the interests of its members, that it was in collusion with the employers, and so on.

It is worthwhile asking, at this juncture, why, if many members were discontented with the policy being adopted by the national leadership of the Transport and General Workers' Union over decasualisation, attempts were not made to change the policy through the normal constitutional machinery? The first part of the answer to this question must be that some such attempts were made. A number have been noted. For example, initially the Glasgow dockers pursued their case through the constitutional machinery of the union in the late 1920's, taking their argument to the national delegate conference; in the early 1930's an attempt was made to raise the issue of joint control at the national delegate conference; and at the time of the discussions over the 1965 Devlin report, dockers who felt that nationalisation should be a prerequisite for decasualisation attempted to ensure that official union policy followed this line. However, while such examples can be highlighted it is also clear that frequently the constitutional machinery was not used. The explanation for this revolves around a number of factors. First, it was clear to all members that any attempts to change union policy in relation to the overall aim of decasualisation was likely to be strongly attacked by the national leadership, and that the national leadership held a considerable advantage when it came to major policy discussions of this kind. It is very rare indeed for the national executive to be defeated on a major policy issue at the national delegate conference: this applies not simply as far as matters relating to dockers are concerned, but also for the rest of the membership. The strategy adopted by dissenting groups within the union, therefore, often was to plead for flexibility in national policy to allow for local variations, rather than to challenge policy "head on", though it should be recorded that usually even this strategy failed, for frequently the union leadership was concerned that local variations would be used by employers to break a policy. The second factor to be considered is that in many cases dockers seemed to react to the implications of policy rather than to general decisions themselves. Of course, this was not always the case (the example of the priority to be given to nationalisation in the mid-1960's is a case in point), but in most instances it was. In this context it might be noted that often it was the involvement of union officials in the disciplining of union members that aroused real anger, rather than the general policy of joint control, and that it was the implications of the priority given by the national union leadership to the preservation of the Dock Labour Scheme in the late 1940's and 1950's, and the view that members must abide by unpopular agreement (such as on overtime), rather than the policy to support the Scheme as such, to which members objected. Consequently, the disputes between members and leaders often arose over particular local issues, and to the people involved there did not appear to be time to pursue the matter through the constitutional machinery: an immediate solution was sought to what was seen as an immediate problem, and often this meant that an unofficial strike seemed more appropriate than a conference resolution. The third factor to be considered is that much of the discontent was focused on the stance taken by officials. In the Transport and General Workers' Union the national executive have the responsibility for implementing and interpreting policy in between delegate conferences. Although the trade group structure provides a check on action, normally the initiative still lies with the full-time officials and the national executive. In such situations, it is easier to react impulsively and immediately or to leave the organisation, rather than to seek the longer term solution. Certainly, it is easier to do this than to try to defeat union leaders in elections. However, it should be noted that on occasions local opposition to the actions of full-time officials was effective, particularly in the post Second World War period, when a number of local officials were removed from their positions. The success achieved in such matters, though, was concentrated at the local level and even then was limited to specific instances. A final factor to be considered, especially in the 1950's and 1960's, was the availability of alternative organisations through which aims and ideas could be organised. The availability of such organisations meant that there was not the same pressure to ensure that the Transport Workers' Union supported the favoured point of view. In a number of cases, it seems to have been felt that it was easier to pursue a policy through another organisation than to try to get the Transport Workers' Union to change its stance.

In summary, then, what can be argued then is that at times members in a number of ports, or sections of the membership, seem to have opposed union policy on decasualisation. The strength or extent of the opposition can be debated, but there is little doubt that such opposition existed, and at certain times was vocal and influential. However, it is more difficult to argue that such opposition had any significant effect on the policy adopted by the national leadership of the Transport and General Workers' Union on decasualisation. It can be pointed out that in certain instances the national executive of the union decided not to push their particular policies as hard as they might have done in an attempt to avoid conflict. For example, at the height of the dispute in Glasgow over registration the national executive suggested that it would not try to force its views on the men in that port. In fact, that "strategic withdrawal" failed because the conflict was far too advanced and the Glasgow dockers' leaders believed that the issue had to be pushed to a conclusion. The same kind of concession was not offered on many occasions, and certainly the overall policy seemed to be unaffected.

How, then, can one explain the relative consistency of the policy adopted by the Transport and General Workers' Union over decasualisation? Why did the expressions of dissatisfaction from members not lead to a change in that policy?

At the outset, one has to recognise that the answer simply might be that the dissatisfaction was not sufficiently widespread to persuade leaders of the Transport and General Workers' Union that changes should be made. It has been admitted already that an assessment of this issue is difficult. The evidence is just not available to enable one to say whether at any particular point in time, say, a majority of docker members of the Transport and General Workers' Union were in favour or opposed to the policy being pursued. Nevertheless, evidence has been presented of persistent dissatisfaction and crucial decisions were taken to form breakaway or rival organisations. Even if such evidence does not imply a majority view on a particular policy issue, it clearly indicates open conflict within the Union. At least one might argue that at first sight it is surprising that union leaders did not seriously consider varying union policy on decasualisation in such circumstances. In practice, it will be argued that if one is seeking an explanation for the consistency of the Transport and General Workers' Union's policy on decasualisation, anyway, one needs to look beyond simply the strength of membership dissatisfaction: that may be one factor to be taken into account, but it is not the only one.

One of the other factors that needs to be examined is the interpretation placed by the leadership of the Transport and General Workers' Union on the actions of docker members. On occasions members claimed that they were opposing union officials, leaving the union, or forming a rival organisation because of dissatisfaction with union policy over decasualisation and its implications. However, what matters in this context is not what the members concerned said was the cause of their action, or what an external observer might suggest was the cause of their action, but what the union leaders themselves believed it to be, for, even assuming that the leaders wanted to remedy the issue causing conflict (and as will be argued later this was not always the case), they would only take action over the issue that they believed was the cause of the conflict, and this might be different from other interpretations. Two examples can be used to illustrate this point.

The first example is taken from the dispute over registration at Glasgow in the 1920's. The establishment of the Anti-Registration League brought correspondence between the Area and the National Headquarters of the union. The view was clearly stated that the size of the rebellion had been overstated, and that many of those who had joined the League had done so as the result of intimidation rather than real disagreement with the policy over registration. Thus, the Scottish Area Secretary told Bevin in a letter that the claims of the Anti-Registration League were overstated and the rank and file docker had been misled by troublemakers.

> Personally, I am of the opinion that the claim of the Anti-Registration League to have 2,000 members is an overrated one. I think that if we divided that number by two, we would then be giving a more accurate statement of the members, and the biggest proportion of this number would be made up of men who had joined the League through intimidation. In fact, when this Registration League was inaugurated and men approached to join it, cards were handed out without any payment, but simply on a promise to pay, and it is certainly true to say that dozens of them never did pay anything.

He went on to argue that the trouble might have "fizzled out" if "anything like strong measures been taken". Rather than suggesting a change of policy, he agreed that failure to enforce existing policy strongly enough "allowed those at the head of the disruptive movement to increase the discontent"[12]. In practice, even the external observer might have some difficulty disentangling the causes of the conflict at Glasgow, for, as has been noted earlier, they appear to have been complex and longstanding. Nevertheless, the point is that the external observer's perception is not what matters; the critical issue is the view of the officials and, in this case, they did not see registration as the real cause of the problem.

The second example is taken from a later period. Throughout the 1950s there were skirmishes between the national leaders of the Transport and General Workers' Union and sections of the membership: these skirmishes led to the establishment of a semi-permanent unofficial movement and the extension of the National Amalgamated Stevedores and Dockers union into Northern ports. They were also, more generally, one of the reasons for the reduction in the number of members of the Transport and General Workers' Union docks section. Some of the people who left the union joined a rival but many others, despite the fact that in many ports there was supposed to be a "closed shop", simply ceased to be a member of any union. The union members involved in the conflicts with the national leadership of the Transport and General Workers' Union, complained about many different items, including a range of policy issues (some, though not all, relating to decasualisation). The national leadership of the Transport and General Workers' Union was not unconcerned about such developments and on occasions took action designed to remedy faults. However, because the national leadership believed that the problem was really one of weaknesses in the administrative machinery of the union in certain ports and individual "trouble makers", it took action to deal with these issues rather than change policy[13]. Again, it does not matter in this context whether the assessment of the national leadership of the Transport and General Workers' Union was right or wrong: what matters is that they believed their own assessment to be correct and took action on that basis.

Another element in the explanation is that the leaders of the Transport and General Workers' Union were concerned about the effect and the interpretation that would be placed on any concessions they made to rank and file dock workers' pressure. For example, Bevin's position with regard to the Scottish dockers was clearly influenced by the fear that his actions might be misinterpreted. In a letter to the Scottish Area Secretary, Bevin reviewed a series of possible reactions to the Glasgow dockers' decision to set up the Anti-Registration League and indicated his concern that if he responded to their actions directly they might believe "they were having an influence on us"[14]. Bevin was also afraid that if one section was allowed to develop a policy of their own, others would follow and by the desire to maintain one national policy. Thus Bullock writes:

> It is easy to represent this episode (the conflict with the Glasgow dockers) as a defence of democratic self-government against the tyranny of a trade union bureaucracy out of touch with the rank-and-file members of the organisation. But Bevin, the General Executive and the National Docks Group Committee saw the issue differently. Bevin never forgot the lesson he had learned in the old Transport Workers' Federation, that particularism was the curse of trade unionism and national action the only effective means of improving the dockers' position. The employers argued, just as the mineowners did, that local variations made a national agreement impracticable. Bevin fought this view at the time of the Shaw Inquiry and experience strengthened his convictions that the only way to get rid of the evils of casual employment was by a comprehensive scheme applied nationally. He knew perfectly well that he had to fight ignorance, prejudice and conservatism on his own side. The action of the Glasgow branch played into the local employers' hands; if other ports claimed the same freedom to make local arrangements as they wished, the chance of a national agreement would be lost.[15]

The union leaders, of course, were not just concerned about dock workers: they were just as concerned about the effect that any "concessions" they might make to groups of dockers might have on other sections of the union's membership. Although dockers had been one of the main groups originally forming the union, subsequent further amalgamations widened the coverage of this union greatly. This meant that the loss of dock membership might be undesirable, but certainly not disastrous. In practice the docks membership was only a fraction, and over the years a declining fraction, of the union's total membership. Many of the other trade groups were much more important in numerical terms - for example, by the end of the interwar period Road Passenger Transport was able to claim almost twice as many members as the docks, and the metal engineering and chemical group had advanced past the dockers' total. In later years, the dockers relative position declined even further. This is not to argue that national leaders were not concerned about the loss of dock members: the docks section always had played an important role in the union, far beyond its sheer numbers. Nevertheless, the loss of members in some ports clearly did not threaten the overall viability of the union. Linked to this is the central argument that the national leadership was concerned not to set an unwelcome precedent for other sections of the union. The docks section was by no means the only one to "cause trouble" and a number of national leaders appear to have taken the view that if they "appeased" dissident dockers they would be encouraging similar action in other sections of the union.

However, an attempt to understand why the national officials of the Transport and General Workers' Union did not change course on their policies over decasualisation needs to look at factors other than simply the extent of pressure from the membership, perceptions of it, and its likely influence. It is also important to take into account the strength of feeling of the leadership of the union, and in particular, the view that they should maintain the course decided upon because it was in the best interests of the dock workers. Earlier, reference was made to the extent to which decasualisation almost became an "article of faith" within the union. In some ways, it gained its own motivating force. Reference was also made to the way in which decasualisation could be used to help the union reinforce its control over the industry. However, the stress on this view of matters should not deflect attention from the genuine belief of many of those putting forward the policy in its value for the docks membership. In this case, we are not simply talking about the various general secretaries of the unions but also about other senior officials including national docks officers. The view was one which in many cases had been developed as the consequences of personal experience in the industry. Little more needs to be said of the strength of feeling of such people on this issue, for it has been mentioned a number of times already, though maybe what is worthwhile stressing, is that this implies that some union leaders maintained an attachment to causes. They did not simply bend with the prevailing view, but held to their "beliefs" despite the unpopularity that doing so brought. Decasualisation, then, was viewed as a "cause" worth fighting for, even if the fight might be costly in terms of support for the union and personal popularity. Further, often it was believed that at the end of the day, the wisdom of the course of action would be appreciated. For example, Deakin firmly believed that the dockers in the northern ports who left the Transport Workers to join the Stevedores union would eventually realise that the policy pursued had been in their own best interests and would return to the Transport Workers. Thus, Allen said:

> The events of the few months before he died (the loss of dockers in the Northern ports to the NASD) saddened Arthur Deakin; he was a tired, sick man nearing retirement, and from his point in life the act of secession had a flavour of ungraciousness about it. He had been long enough at the head of affairs in the Union to look upon criticisms of the Union as personal affronts. Deakin felt that his Union was in the right and that eventually the Northern dockers who had joined the Stevedores' union would realise this and return.[16]

Of course, not everyone concerned viewed decasualisation in this light, but a number did, and it is a factor that needs to be taken into account in any assessment of events.

The argument being put forward, then, is that the national leaders of the Transport and General Workers' Union maintained a consistent policy on decasualisation, despite on occasions evidence of dissatisfaction from sections of the membership. They did so, partly because they did not believe that the majority of their members really opposed the policy (and it has been suggested that whether this belief was a correct or incorrect assessment is relatively unimportant), partly because they believed that they could not "appease" one section of the union without this affecting the attitude of members in other sections and partly because they were convinced that decasualisation was an important development which would benefit their members and was worthwhile fighting misguided members as well as governments and employers for.

Notes

1. The MacLean Committee met and produced reports in 1924 and then was reconvened in 1930.
2. For example, the Transport and General Workers' Union attempted to link the deliberations of the Blanesborough Committee to their policies on decasualisation and maintenance.
3. V Allen, *Trade Union Leadership*, Longman, London, 1957, p183.
4. Ministry of Labour, *Final Report of the Committee of Inquiry into Certain Matters Concerning the Port Transport Industry*, HMSO, London, 1965, Cmnd 2734.
5. This statement is not simply based on documentary evidence, but was confirmed as being the position during the 1950s by people who were senior national officials in the Transport and General Workers' Union at the time.
6. Court of Inquiry into Transport Workers, HMSO, London, 1920, Cd 93617.
7. This is brought out clearly by A Bullock in, *The Life and Times of Ernest Bevin*, Vol 1, Heinemann, London, 1964.
8. Ibid.
9. T Evans, *Bevin*, Allen & Unwin, London, 1946, p15.
10. See, V Allen, *Op Cit*.
11. B Shenfield, *Security of Employment: A Study in the Construction Industry*, PEP, London, 1968.
12. Letter dated 29 June 1928.
13. Discussion with a former senior national official of the Transport and General Workers' Union brought out that in the 1950s the problems being faced on the docks were perceived largely as resulting from organisational difficulties. One result of this perception was that organisational changes were made: for example, Tom Cronin was moved to take charge of matters at the Hull docks.
14. Letter dated 28 June 1928.
15. A Bullock, *Op Cit*, pp 467-468.
16. *Op Cit*, p207.

8 Policy making in trade unions: a review

Rank and file union members who are dissatisfied with union policy have a number of means open to them through which they can challenge that policy. For example, they can use the machinery that enables them to propose resolutions for debate at the national conference, or they may challenge particular leaders who have been supporting the disliked policy and seek to defeat them in an election. The literature on internal union democracy shows divergent views about the likely success of attempts to use the constitutional machinery in this way. However, most writers recognise some limitations: rank and file members who oppose a policy may be disorganised, have little in the way of the administrative expertise and finance necessary to mount an effective campaign, and may lack adequate access to channels of communications or if they can gain access to them, they may find difficulty using them convincingly. The differences that can be noted in the literature centre on whether problems such as these effectively form a barrier that prevents rank and file membership from challenging policy, or whether they are simply problems that, on occasions, can be overcome.

It is clear, however, that if rank and file members, for whatever reasons, fail to overturn the policy decisions through constitutional mechanisms (and the failure simply may be the result of the fact that they only represent a minority, albeit a significant minority, point of view), then this is not necessarily an end to the matter. They can continue their opposition through nonconstitutional means (for example, by ignoring official policy, and if necessary striking to oppose it) and ultimately they may decide to leave the union, either simply by allowing their membership to lapse or by joining a rival organisation. Such action has been seen as representing a major challenge to union leaders. It has been suggested, for example, that union leaders cannot simply sit and watch disaffected members leave, and, say, set up or join rival organisations: eventually they will be forced to take some action if only to defend their own organisation and th ir own position within it. However, within this general statement, a number of questions remain. When should union leaders become concerned that members might leave? What signs should they look for? Are sustained policy disagreements a warning sign that the alert union leader should notice? Alternatively, is some kind of unofficial action, or membership resignation to join another organisation the occasion when real concern should be shown? In the same kind of fashion, how many members have to leave or show that they are disaffected before union leaders "must" take notice? In the case most frequently cited, that of the North American union leader John L Lewis, the decline in membership took place over a period of years and by the time Lewis took action to reverse the trend, the union was less than a fifth of the size it had been when Lewis was elected President. Similarly, the literature does not give guidance on what kind of action union leaders will take in the face of the threat or actual loss of members. Will they try to placate the members in an effort to persuade them to return to the union, or simply tighten up the organisation to enable it to fight a breakaway effectively? It might be argued that John L Lewis, by changing policy tried (and in these terms successfully) to placate the membership. However, by no means all union leaders have taken this path.

An examination of the case of the Transport and General Workers' Union's policy on moves to decasualise dock labour does not provide answers to such questions which can be applied, in the form of a general rule, to all unions. Nevertheless, this case does provide further insight into the issues raised and insight which can be used to further elaborate possible reactions in other cases. Essentially it gives a guide to the kind of factors that need to be looked at and the kind of factors that are likely to influence the action taken. The result, then, is not a general theory, but more of an indicator of important areas that need examination. The discussion might be divided into two parts. The first will deal with membership loss, and the second with the reactions of leaders. The concentration on membership loss in the first part is not meant to imply that conflict between union leaders and members which does not at least threaten such an outcome is unimportant; clearly this is not the case. Nevertheless, the threat of membership loss, or actual memberships loss, is seen by many writers as an important focus for pressure and is being used as a basis for discussion, even though some of the points raised may have relevance to less openly serious situations.

Membership Loss

It is clear that there is no major cut off point, either in terms of the kind of action that might be seen as an indicator of possible membership loss or in terms of the numbers/percentage of membership loss after which leaders will decide that they must take some kind of action. In some cases indications of majority and minority positions may be important, in others they may be less crucial. Different leaderships will react to similar issues or threats of loss in different kinds of ways. There are, however, a number of factors that might be seen as important in influencing reactions in such matters.

The first factor is the visibility of events. If the threat of, rather than actual, membership loss is the matter of concern, then clearly there are major differences in the visibility of different kinds of action. Opposition to policy which leads to a major unofficial strike will be highly visible, though some unofficial action may pass unnoticed at the level of the national executive committee of the union and more passing opposition may be noticed by few outside the group directly concerned. If membership loss is not simply threatened but actually occurs, then other issues affect visibility. Many unions regularly face a substantial turnover of members. In part this is related to members changing jobs. In a general union, like the Transport and General Workers' Union, the normal turnover of members is very high and it will not always be easy to detect a small increase in the number of members leaving a union because of dissatisfaction with policy or performance. In many unions anyway the monitoring of membership changes is far from precise and certainly not up to date: it may be, therefore, a while before changes in the level of membership even come to the attention of national union leaders. In the Transport and General Workers' Union membership figures are regularly reported by trade groups, but there is a time lag especially between membership lapses (rather than resignations) and their appearance in such figures.

These detailed considerations, though, are transformed, if membership loss occurs in a highly publicised fashion and are directed specifically against the established policy of the union. In the case of the Transport and General Workers' Union's policy over decasualisation, the formation of the breakaway Scottish Transport and General Workers' Union and the loss of membership in northern ports to the National Amalgamated Stevedores and Dockers union were examples of highly visible and well publicised membership losses. They were losses about which union leaders were well aware and which they could not ignore. In percentage terms they represented a very small loss compared to the overall membership of the union, and even compared to the membership of the docks section, they were far from catastrophic. Nevertheless, they were concentrated and seen as a direct challenge and it was this, rather than the size of the membership loss, that was important.

A second factor that needs to be taken into account in discussing membership loss is the structure of the union. General unions, like the Transport and General Workers' Union, are built around a variety of different membership centres. Membership loss which results from a policy or actions affecting just one such centre may be sustained to a greater extent than would be the case in a different kind of situation. In this sense, general unions are much more robust than, say, industrial unions for even the total loss of members from one industry or trade may not threaten the viability of the union as a whole. In the case of the Transport and General Workers' Union, had all its docker members left and joined the National Amalgamated Stevedores and Dockers union, the size of the union, relatively, would have been little changed and union leaders would still have had a union to lead. Of course, certain union leaders (particularly the national docks officer) would have faced difficulties, but it is at least conceivable that he could have been transferred to other work. If the example were turned round, however, the position would be very different. The leaders of the National Amalgamated Stevedores and Dockers union would have found that they had no union to lead (just as seemed likely in the case of John L Lewis) if all of their members in the ports had left and joined the Transport and General Workers' Union.

The above is not meant to suggest that the loss of a section of the membership in the way described would be disregarded. In the instance quoted clearly this would not have been the case. The loss or the threat of a loss of a section of membership obviously would create tensions and raise questions about the running of the union, though there might be instances when the national leadership could survive such a situation; for example, if there was an open split between the interests of one section of the union and the rest of the members, and the union leaders could be seen to be supporting the majority. In the case of the dockworkers and the Transport and General Workers' Union, however, it is clear that whatever the circumstances, the loss of the dockers' section would have been seen as a major blow, because dock workers were instrumental in establishing the union and have played a major role ever since. The loss of the docks section would have been a major psychological blow, rather than one which could have been assessed in numerical terms, and in practice, it is doubtful if such a loss could have been contemplated. Such considerations have general as well as specific relevance. Nevertheless, despite such important caveats, the general point that the effect of the threat or actual membership loss may, to some extent, be influenced by the structure of the union remains.

Reaction of Union Leaders

The reaction of union leaders to evidence of discontent amongst rank and file members may take a number of different forms. The form it takes may be influenced by the strength and nature of the discontent. However, it will also be influenced by a number of other factors more directly associated with the leaders themselves.

One such factor is perception of union leaders of the nature of the problem. In the discussion of the case of dock workers in the Transport and General Workers' Union it was pointed out that on one occasion union leaders interpreted discontent as being the result of organisational rather than policy disagreements when other assessments could have been made. On another occasion in this instance, the post-war unofficial strikes, the General Secretary of the Transport Union claimed that the real cause of the trouble was politically motivated individuals. At the union's 1948 Scottish Conference, Denham claimed that 36 or the 48 members of the unofficial committee organising the Zinc Oxide strike were either communists or "fellow travellers". More generally, frequently leaders of organisations claim that their policies would attract maximum support but are not doing so because they are not properly understood. In these terms the problem is not the policy but the means of communications. They may also on occasions blame a small group of malcontents who they believe are misleading members and arguing that the solution to the problem lies in dealing with the malcontents rather than changing policy. The important issue to be stressed is that in any assessment of what action is likely to be taken by leaders as the result of evidence of discontent on the part of members, the crucial factor is not what the members themselves say is the issue at stake, nor what an outside observer might assess, but the interpretation placed by the people who are going to take decisions on the matter.

Another factor to be taken into account is the position of the national leaders vis-a-vis their union: for example, the extent of the power held by the union leaders. Some leaders like, in the case of the Transport and General Workers' Union discussed, Bevin, have enormous power which rests not simply on their formal position, but more specifically on the prestige the individual has built up. Such leaders are aware that in a confrontation they have a major advantage. It is an advantage that they can use to try to defeat opposition, though on other occasions they may feel that it enables them to make a conciliatory gesture. In essence they are much more likely to be able to take the initiative and are less likely to be concerned about detailed adverse reaction than union leaders in other situations would be. A further factor to be taken into account concerns the perception of the union leader or the likely consequence of any action they might take. The case of dock workers and the Transport and General Workers' Union showed that, for example, in that instance, the union leaders were not simply interested in the effect of their actions on the union members expressing dissatisfaction, but were more centrally interested on the effect of their actions on other sections of the union. A trade union leader, if he or she is concerned with their position in the union, and with the maintenance of the organisation, must take a broad view of the consequences of his or her actions. A concession to one group, thus, may not be seen as a magnanimous or healing gesture by other sections of the union, but as a sign of weakness, and it may be that for this reason, rather than any other, that a union leader decides it has to be avoided.

In the same way, a union leader will be concerned not simply with the impression his or her actions are likely to give inside the union, but will also be concerned with the impression gained outside. Deakin, for example, in his dealings with dock workers, often pressed his members to abide by agreements even if they (and sometimes he) disliked them, partly because he did not want to give anyone ammunition that might be used against the 1947 Dock Labour Scheme. Another element behind his approach on this matter, though, was that he felt, more generally, that it was important that union leaders should be seen to honour agreements. If a contrary impression were created, then this might adversely affect a leader's ability to operate on behalf of the union and negotiate agreements in the future which might be to the benefit of union members. Thus, one commentator has argued that no attempt was made by Deakin to outbid the other organisations that sought the loyalty of the dockers, because to do so might have meant on occasions authorising the violation of voluntary agreements, and, for Deakin, that would have been sacrilege. Speaking in the union's 1949 conference, Deakin said that the violation of an agreement was not just a question affecting the docker, it was "a question as to whether or not we are people who having signed an agreement and having accepted a procedure for the settlement of disputes are going to carry out our obligations".[1]

It is also important when discussing the reactions of union leaders to take one other factor into account; the strength of the beliefs and commitment of the leader concerned. Trade union leaders are often protrayed cynically as little more than "organisation men": they started their own union careers holding certain ideals and saw themselves as being able to make significant changes that would improve the position of rank and file members, but such straightforward ideals and objectives have long since been discarded. This can have happened for one of a number of different reasons: their own career and status may have become bound up with the organisation so that they may be more concerned with the survival of the organisation as such, rather than with the attainment of specific objectives, or they may have been seduced away from their original ideals because of the extent to which they have become part of the "establishment" (through service on official committees and the like) and because of the extent of their contacts with employers, or they may more simply have become too concerned with details and techniques and have lost sight of original objectives. There is little doubt that in some cases these images of the trade union leader may be correct. There are obviously pressures and temptations which make it likely that some leaders may lose sight of the reasons behind their original involvement with the union. Nevertheless, if such a view were put forward as a general rule then it would be misleading. The pressures should not be seen as determinants. The case of the Transport and General Workers' Union's policy on the decasualisation of dock labour showed that many national leaders (Bevin is the best, but by no means the only, example) retained commitments to specific causes. In this sense one of the popular views of union leaders frequently expressed in the media, which sees them as being dedicated to specific (usually, from the point of view of the reporter, undesirable) causes, and willing to use any means to achieve them, may have as much validity as the more common academic view of union leaders as "organisation men". In practice, neither view is correct as a general rule. Union leaders differ enormously: few are untouched by their rise to power but many retain an attachment to more than simply maintaining their own position. A view of union leaders needs to present balance and variety. In terms of the central question at hand, clearly the extent to which a union leader maintains an attachment to causes, and to a specific cause in dispute, will be an important influence on action.

A More Flexible Approach

The view being put forward here is not that one can identify particular determinants of the way policy will be made in trade unions. Factors which are likely to influence the strength of particular sources of pressure have been highlighted in an attempt to show the kind of things that need to be looked at rather than to predict particular outcomes.Policy making in trade unions, and the relationship between union leaders and members, needs to be approached in a flexible and pragmatic fashion. Case studies will be able to show us how mechanisms work. Particular organisational arrangements might be seen as encouraging or inhibiting particular kinds of action. Particular levels and kinds of actions on the part of rank and file union members may be likely to bring forward certain kinds of reactions from union leaders and thus influence policy. The importance of such issues should not be underestimated. However, at the same time, the importance of such issues should not be overestimated. Organisational arrangements may strongly influence the direction of action but will not determine it, just as particular levels and kind of membership action may influence the way leaders react and policy but not determine it. Organisational arrangements and membership reaction are not the only important factors: the interpretation, position, and strength of commitment of the union leader is also important. They may perceive and approach similar situations in different ways; they may react to the same challenge in different ways.

At the end of the day, then, there is no particular generally applicable model for policy making in trade unions which is able to specify outcomes of disagreements or conflicts between union leaders and members. Such conflicts may be resolved in a variety of different fashions, and their resolution will depend on action and reaction between members and leaders, on changing balances of power, and on different interpretations of situations. Neither members nor leaders simply reflect the organisational or more general positions: they retain a degree of freedom. The different interpretations and reactions of individuals, both union members and leaders, means that there are many possible outcomes to conflict over policy within unions.

Notes

1   V L Allen, *Trade Union Leadership*, Longman, London, 1957, p207.

Bibliography

Allen, V. L., (1954),*Power in Trade Unions,* Longman, Green & Co., London.
Allen, V. L., (1957),*Trade Union Leadership,* Longman, London.
Anderson, J. A., (1978), A Comparative Analysis of Local Union *Democracy,* Industrial Relations, Vol 17, No.3.
Banks, J. A., (1974), *Trade Unionism,* Collier MacMillan, London.
Barbash, J, (1967), *American Unions,* Random House, New York.
Bealey, F., (1977), *The Political System of the Post Office Engineering Union, British Journal of Industrial Relations, Vol 15, No.3, pp374-395.*
Bean, R., (1985), Custom, Job Regulation and Dock Labour in Liverpool, *International Review of Social History,* Vol XXVII, Part 3.
Bray, M, Davies, E., (Winter 1982), Trade Union Democracy from the Inside: Comparison of the British AUEW and Australian AMWSU, *Industrial Relations Journal,* Vol XIII, No.4.
Broomwich, L., (1959), *Union Constitutions,* The Fund for the Republic, New York.
Bukharin, N., (1925), In *Historical Materialism: A System of Sociology,* International Publishers, New York.
Bullock, A., (1960), *The Life and Times of Ernest Bevin,* Vol 1, Heinemann, London.
Chaison, G. N., Rose, J. B., (May 1977), *Turnover Amongst Presidents of Construction National Unions,* Industrial Relations Journal, Vol 16, No.2.
Child, J., Loveridge, R., Warner, M., (1973), *Towards an Organisational Study of Trade Unions,* Sociology, Vol 7.
Clegg, H. A., (1954), *General Union,* Blackwell, Oxford
Clegg, H. A., Killick, A. J., Adams, R., (1961), *Trade Union Officers,* Blackwell, Oxford.
Cole, G. D. H., (1961), *An Introduction to Trade Unionism,* Allen & Unwin, London.
Coleman, J. R., (1955), *The Compulsive Pressures of Union Democracy,* American Journal of Sociology, Vol 6, No.6.
Court of Inquiry into Transport Workers, HMSO, London. (1920)

Cyriax, G., Oakeshott, R., (1960), *The Bargainers*, Faber, London.

Dahl, R. A., (1958), *A Ctirique of the Ruling Elite Model*, American Political Science Review, Vol 52.

Daniel, W. W., Milward, N., (1983), *Workplace Industrial Relations in Britain*, Heinemann, London.

Dunn, S., Gennard, J., (1984), *The Closed Shop in British Industry*, MacMillan, London.

Davis, E., (1977), *Decision Making in the Australian AMWU*, Industrial Relations, Vol 16, No.2.

Edelstein, J. D., (1967), *An Organisational Theory of Union Democracy*, American Sociological Review, Vol 32.

Edelstein, J., *Democracy in a National Unions The British AEU*, Industrial Relations Journal, Vol 4, No.3.

Edelstein, J. D., Warner, M (1967), *Comparative Union Democracy*, Transaction Books, New Brunswick.

Evans, T., (1946), *Bevin*, Allen & Unwin, London.

Finley, J. E., (1972), *The Corrupt Kingdom*, Simon and Shuster, New York.

Flanders, A., (1968), *Trade Unions*, Hutchinson, London.

Fosh, P., (1981), *The Active Trade Unionist*, Cambridge University Press, Cambridge.

Fox, A., (1972), *A Sociology of Work in Industry*, Collier-MacMillan, London.

Glick, W., Mirvis, P., Harder, D., (1977), *Union Satisfaction and Participation*, Industrial Relations Journal, Vol 16, No.2.

Goldstein, J., (1952), *The Government of a British Trade Union*, Free Press, Glencoe.

Goldthorpe, J. H., Lockwood, D., Bechhofer, Platt, J., (1958), *The Affluent Worker: Industrial Attitudes and Behaviour*, Cambridge University Press, London.

Goodman, J. F. B., Whittingham, T. G., (1969), *Shop Stewards in British Industry*, McGraw-Hill, London

Hall, B. (ed), (1972), *Autocracy and Insurgency in Organized Labour*, Transaction Books, Neww Brunswick.

Hemingway, J., (1978), *Conflict and Democracy: Studies in Trade Union Government*, Oxford University Press, Oxford.

Howells, J. M., Woodfield, A. E., (1970), *The Ability of Managers and Trade Union Officers to Predict Workers' Preferences*, British Journal of Industrial Relations, Vol VIII.

Hughes, J., (1968), *Trade Union Structure and Government*, Research Paper 5, Part 2, Royal Commission on Trade Unions and Employers' Association, 1965-8, HMSO, London.

International Labour Office (1961), *The Trade Union Situation in the United Kingdom*, I.L.O.,Geneva.

Jackson, M. P., (1974), *The Price of Coal*, Croom Helm, London.

James, L., (1981), "Sources of Legitimate Power in Polyarchic Trade Union Government", *Sociology*, Vol 15, No.,2.

Jensen, V. H., (1964), *The Hiring of Dock Workers*, Harvard University Press, Cambridge (Mass).

Kendall, W., (1975), *The Labour Movement in Europe*, Allen Lane, London.

Kerr, C., (1957), *Unions and Union Leaders of Their Own Choosing*, The Fund for the Republic, New York.

Lane, T., (1974), *The Union Makes Us Strong*, Arrow Books, London.

Lascelles, E. C. P., Bullock, S. S., (1924), *Dock Labour and Decasualisation*, P. S. King, London.

Leiserson, W. M., (1959), *American Trade Union Democracy*, Columbia U.P., New York.

Lerner, S. W., (1961), *Breakaway Unions and the Small Trade Union*, Allen & Unwin, London.

Lipset, S. M., Trow, M. A., Coleman (1956), *Union Democracy*, Free Press, New York.

Lumley, R., (1973), *White Collar Unionism in Britain*, Methuen, London.

McCarthy, W. E. J., (1964), *The Closed Shop in Britain*, Blackwell, Oxford.

McCarthy, W. E. J., Porter, S. R., (1968), *Shop Stewards and Workshop Relations*, Royal Commission on Trade Unions and Employers' Associations, 1965-81, Research Paper 10, HMSO, London.

Magrath, C. P., (1958), *Democracy in Overalls: The Futile Quest for Union Democracy*, Industrial and Labour Relations Review, Vol 12.

Martin, R., (1968), "Union Democracy: An Explanatory Framework", *Sociology*, Vol 2.

Mayhew, H., (1861), *London Labour and the London Poor*, Griffin, Brown & Co., London.

Millward, N., Stevens, M., (1968), *British Workplace Industrial Relations 1980-1984*, Gower, Aldershot.

Ministry of Labour, (1941), *Dock Labour in Merseyside, Manachester and Preston areas: Explanatory Memorandum*, HMSO, London.

Ministry of Labour, (1965), *Final Report of the Committee of Inquiry into Certain Matters Concerning the Port Transport* Industry, HMSO, London, Cmnd 2734.

Ministry of Labour, (1937), *Port Labour in Aberdeen and Glasgow: Report of a Board of Enquiry*, HMSO, London.

Ministry of Labour and National Service, (1954), *Final Report of a Court Inquiry into a Disputein the London Docks*, HMSO, London.

Ministry of Labour and National Service, (1946), *Report of the Inquiry held under Paragraph 1(4)of the Schedule to the Dock Workers (Regulation of Employment) Act 1946*, HMSO, London.

Ministry of Labour and National Service, (1946), *Report of a Committee to Inquire into the Operation of the Dock Workers (Regulation of Employment) Scheme*, 1947 HMSO, London, Cmnd 9831.

Ministry of Labour and National Service, (1947), *Report of a Committee of Inquiry into the Amount and Basis of Calculation of the Guaranteed Wage to be made to Dock Workers under the Dock Workers (Regulation of Employment) Scheme*, 1947, HMSO, London.

Ministry of Labour and National Service, (1951), *Report on Certain Aspects of the Manchester (Salford) Dock Strike, April-June 1951*, HMSO, London, Cmd 8375.

Ministry of Labour and National Service, (1951), *Unofficial Stoppages in the London Docks*, HMSO, London.

Moran, M., (1974), *The Union of Post Office Workers: A Study of Political Sociology*, MacMillan, London.

Nicholas, A. W., (1965), "Fractions: A Comparative Analysis", in A S AMonograph, No.2, *Political Systems and the Distribution of Power*, Tavistock, London.

Nicholson, N., Ursell, G., Blyton, P., (1981), *The Dynamics of White Collar Unionism*, Academic Press, London.

Phillips, G., Whiteside, N., (1985), *Casual Employment*, Clarendon Press, Oxford.

Rathbone, E., (1903), *Inquiry into the Conditions of Labour at the Liverpool Docks*, Liverpool Economic and Statistical Society.

Roberts, B. C., (1956), *Trade Union Government and Administration in Great Britain*, Harvard U.P. Cambridge (Mass).

Roberts, B. C., (1952), *Trade Unions in a Free Society*, Hutchinson, London.

Romer, S., (1967), *The International Brotherhood of Treasures*, Wiley, New York, 1967.

Rose, A., (1952), *Union Solidarity*, University of Minesota Press, Minneapolis.

Royal Commission on Unemployment Insurance, (1931), *Report*, HMSO, London.

Sayles, L., Strauss, G., (1953), *The Local Union*, Harcourt Brace, New York.

Seidman, J., London, Karsh, B., Tagliacozzo, D., (1958), *The Workers Views His Union,* University of Chicago Press, Chicago.

Seldman, J., Karsh, B., Tagliacozzo, D., (1956), "A Typology of Rank-and-File Union Members, American Journal of Sociology, Vol 4.

Selznick, P., (1952), *The Orgnaizational Weapon: A Study of Bolshevik Strategy and Tactics,* McGraw-Hill, New York.

Shenfield, B., (1968), *Security of Employment: A Study in the Construction Industry,* PEP, London.

Silverman, D., (1970), *The Theory of Organisations,* Heineman, London.

Simey, T. S., (1956), *The Dock Worker,* Liverpool University Press, Liverpool.

Slichter, S. H., (1947), *Challenge of Industrial Relations,* Cornell University Press, Ithca.

Spinard, W., (1960), *Correlates of Trade Union Participation: A Summary of the Literature,* American Sociological Review, Vol 25.

Steiber, J., 1967, *Governing the U A W, Wiley,* New York.

Strauss, G., May 1977, *Union Government in the US: Research Past, and Future,* Industrial Relations, Vol 16, No.2.

Summers, C, 1952,"Union Democracy and Union Discipline", Proceedings of New York Universities Fifth Annual   Conference on Labour, Matthew Bander, New York.

Taft, P., 1957, "Internal Affairs of Unions and the Taft-Hartley Act", *Industrial and Labour Relations Review,* Vol 11, No.3.

Tannenbaum, A. S., Kahn, R. L., 1958, *Participation in Union Locals,* Row and Peterson, Evanston (Illinois).

Taplin, E., 1986, *The Dockers' Union,* Leicester University Press.

Tunstall, J., 1962, *The Fishermen,* MacGibbon & Kee, London.

Turner, H. A., 1962, *Trade Union Growth, Structure and Policy,* Allen & Unwin, London.

Urwin, H., Murray, C., 1983, "Democracy and Trade Unions", *Industrial Relations Journal,* Vol 14, No.4.

Undy, R., Martin, R., 1982, *Ballots and Trade Union Democracies,* Blackwell, Oxford.

Undy, R., "The Electoral Influence of the Opposition Party in the AUEW Engineering", British Journal of Industrial Relations, Vol XV11, No.1.

Warner, M., 1973, *Industrial Conflict Revisited,* in M. Warner (ed), *The Sociology of the Workplace,* Allen & Unwin, London.

Webb, S. & B., 1909, *The Minority Report of the Poor Law Commission,* Longman, Green & Co., London.

Wilders, M. G., Parker, S. R., 1975, *Changes in Workplace Industrial Relations,* 1966-72, British Journal of Industrial Relations, Vol X111, No.1.

Wootton, G., June 1961, *Parties in Union Government: the AESD,* Political Studies, Vol 9.

Wright-Mills, C., 1948, *The New Men of Power,* Harcourt Brace, New York.

Wright-Mllls, C., 1959, *The Power Elite,* Oxford University Press, New York.

Index